Language Arts
Workbook B

Siegfried Engelmann
Jean Osborn
Karen Davis
Evan Haney
Owen Engelmann

Acknowledgments

The authors are grateful to the following people for their assistance in the preparations of Reading Mastery Transformations Grade K Language.

Cally Dwyer
Katherine Gries
Debbi Kleppen
Patricia McFadden
Melissa Morrow

mheducation.com/prek-12

Copyright © 2021 McGraw-Hill Education

All rights reserved. No part of this publication may be reproduced or distributed in any form or by any means, or stored in a database or retrieval system, without the prior written consent of McGraw-Hill Education, including, but not limited to, network storage or transmission, or broadcast for distance learning.

Send all inquiries to:
McGraw-Hill Education
8787 Orion Place
Columbus, OH 43240

ISBN: 978-0-07-905555-2
MHID: 0-07-905555-9

Printed in the United States of America.

2 3 4 5 6 7 8 9 10 LMN 26 25 24 23 22 21

_____

three   bricks   funny
good   straw   sticks   scary

This story is about _____ pigs and a wolf.

First the wolf blows down the house made of _____.

Next the wolf blows down the house made of _____.

Last the three pigs hide in the house made of _____.

This was a _____ story.

Side 2

? ? ? ? ? ?

Side 2

???????

1. How old is the cat
2. The dog was playing
3. I like trees
4. Was the grass green

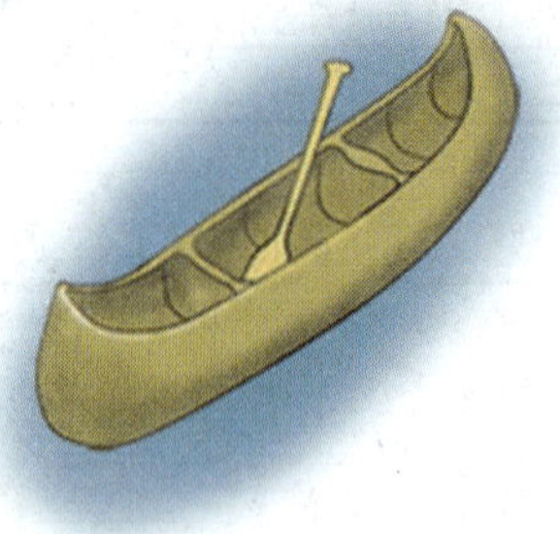

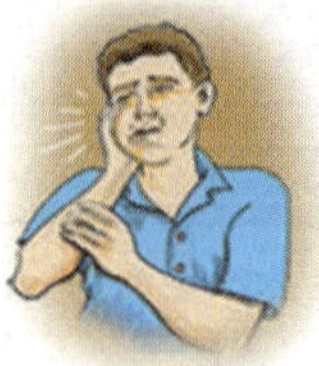

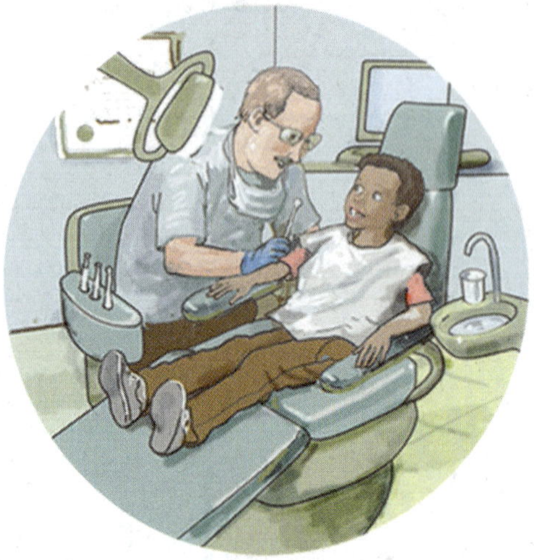

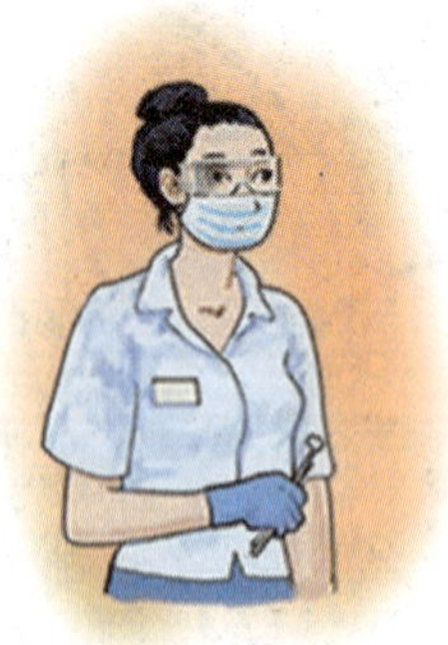

Side 2

1. The wave was big
2. Are your socks tan
3. Who made that kite
4. I can see a crow
5. How big is that bird

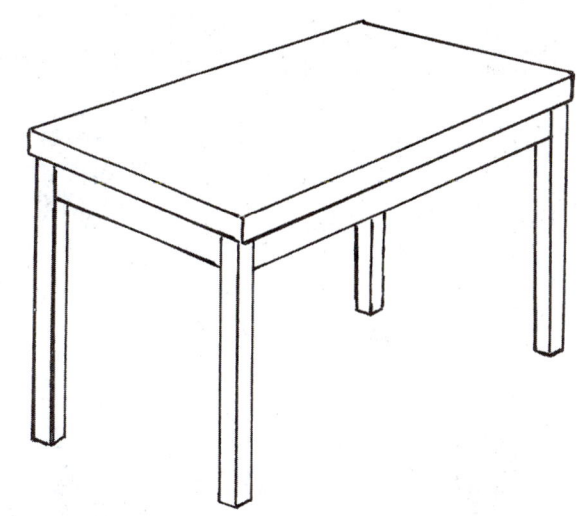

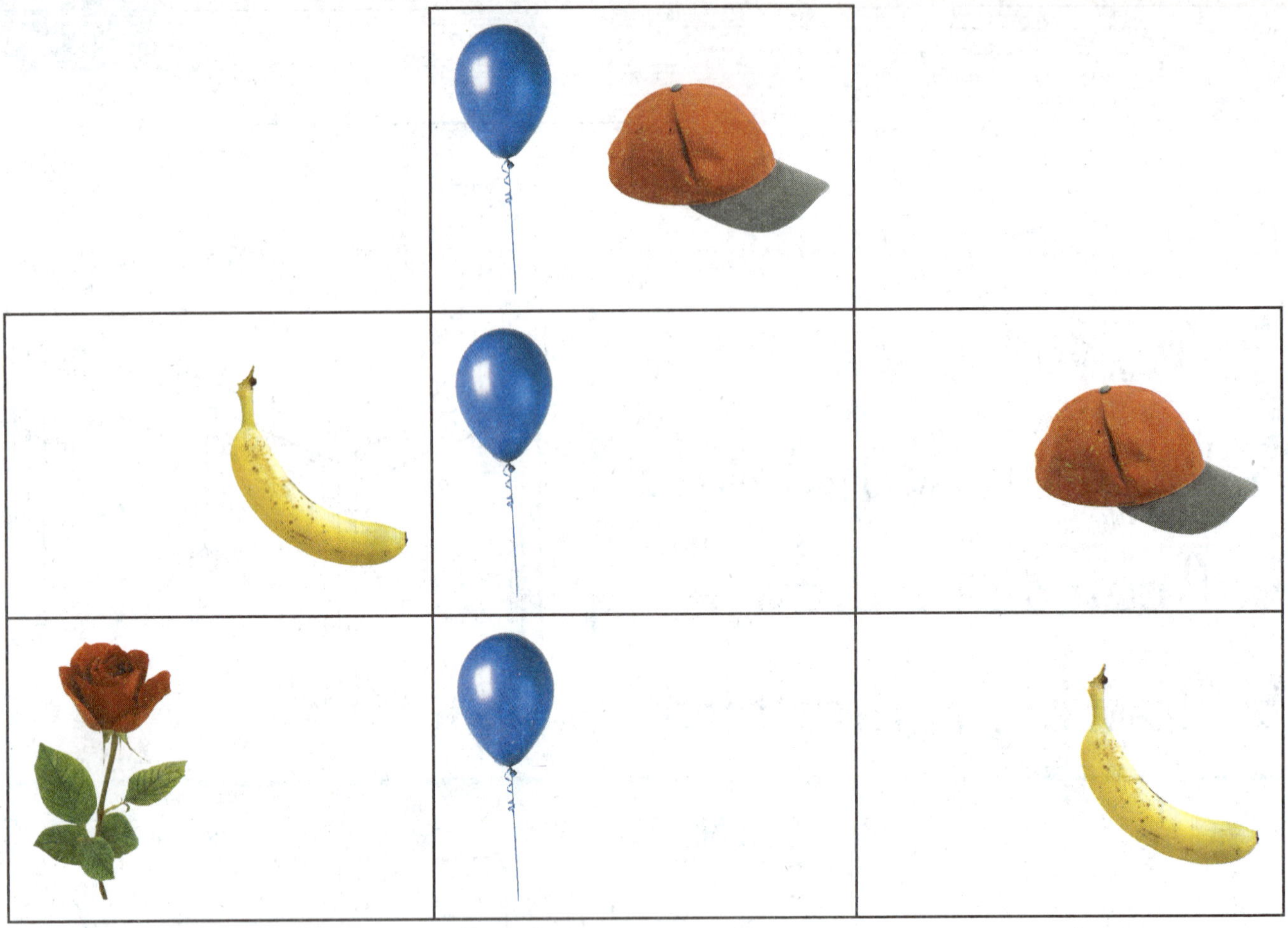

Side 2

1. I will not go to the store

2. My hat is brown

3. Did you see a turtle

4. Why did that car stop

5. Pam is sick

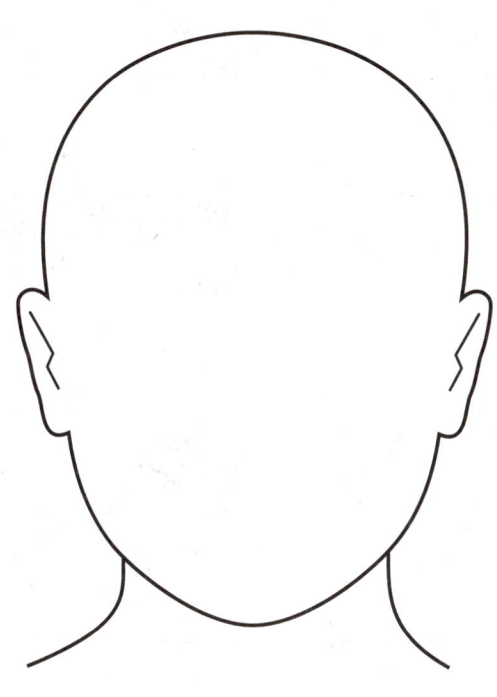

Side 2

_____

- - - - - - - - - - - - - - -

_____

> not   princess   sad
> Timmy   happy   good   mother

This story is about a boy named
_____
- - - - - - - - - - - - - - -
_____ .

_____
- - - - - - -
His _____ thought the rabbit was just a toy.

_____
- - - - - - -
A _____ told him the toy rabbit was real.

I think the rabbit in the woods was
_____
- - - - - - -
_____ .

- - - - - - -
This was a _____ story.

Side 1

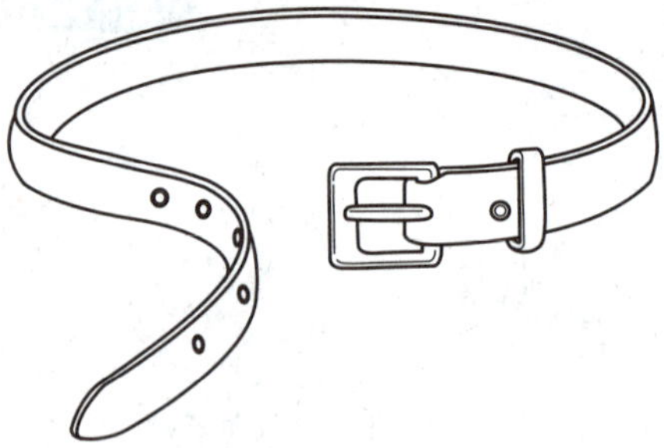

Side 2

87

Side 1

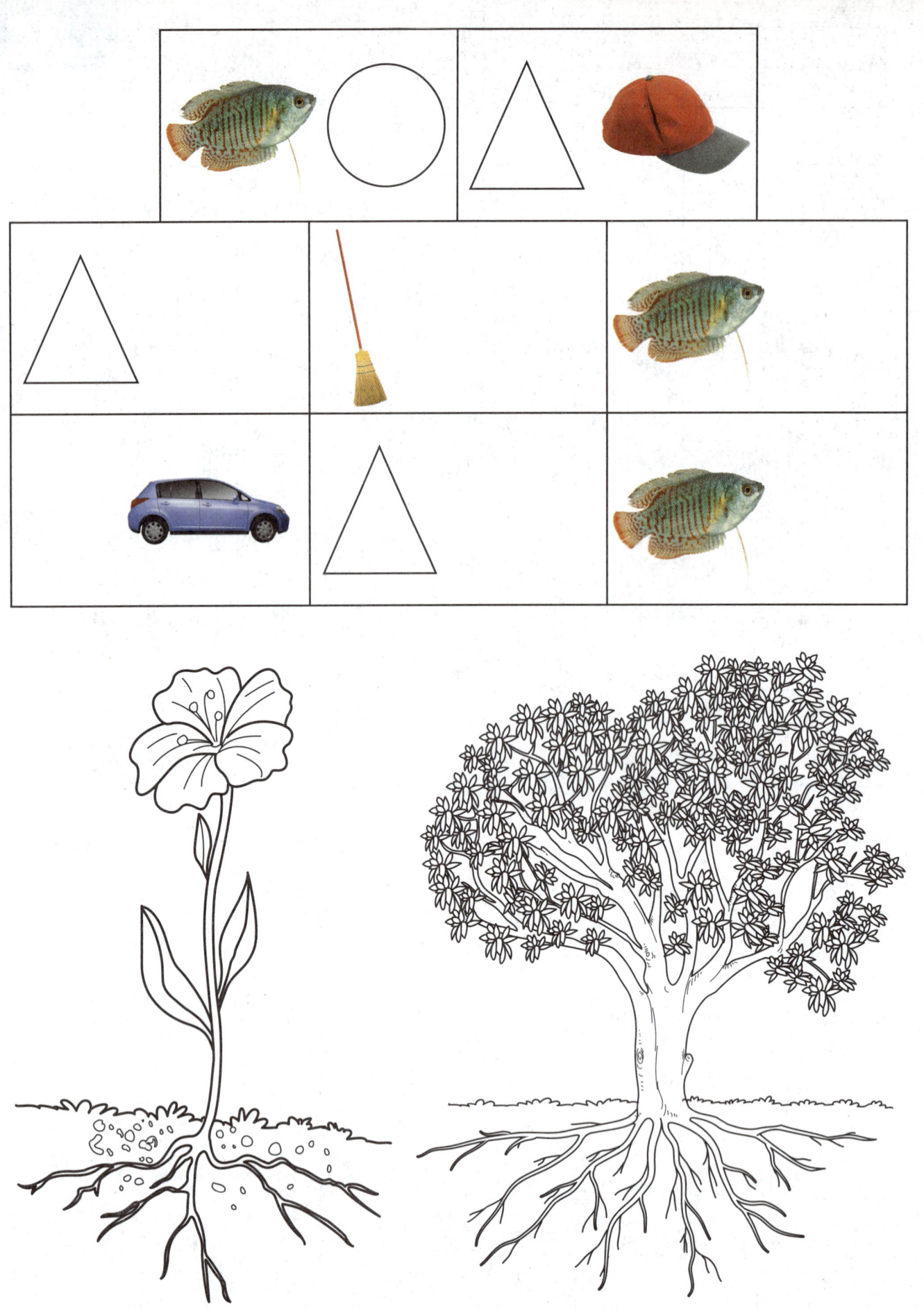

Side 2

88

Side 1

Side 2

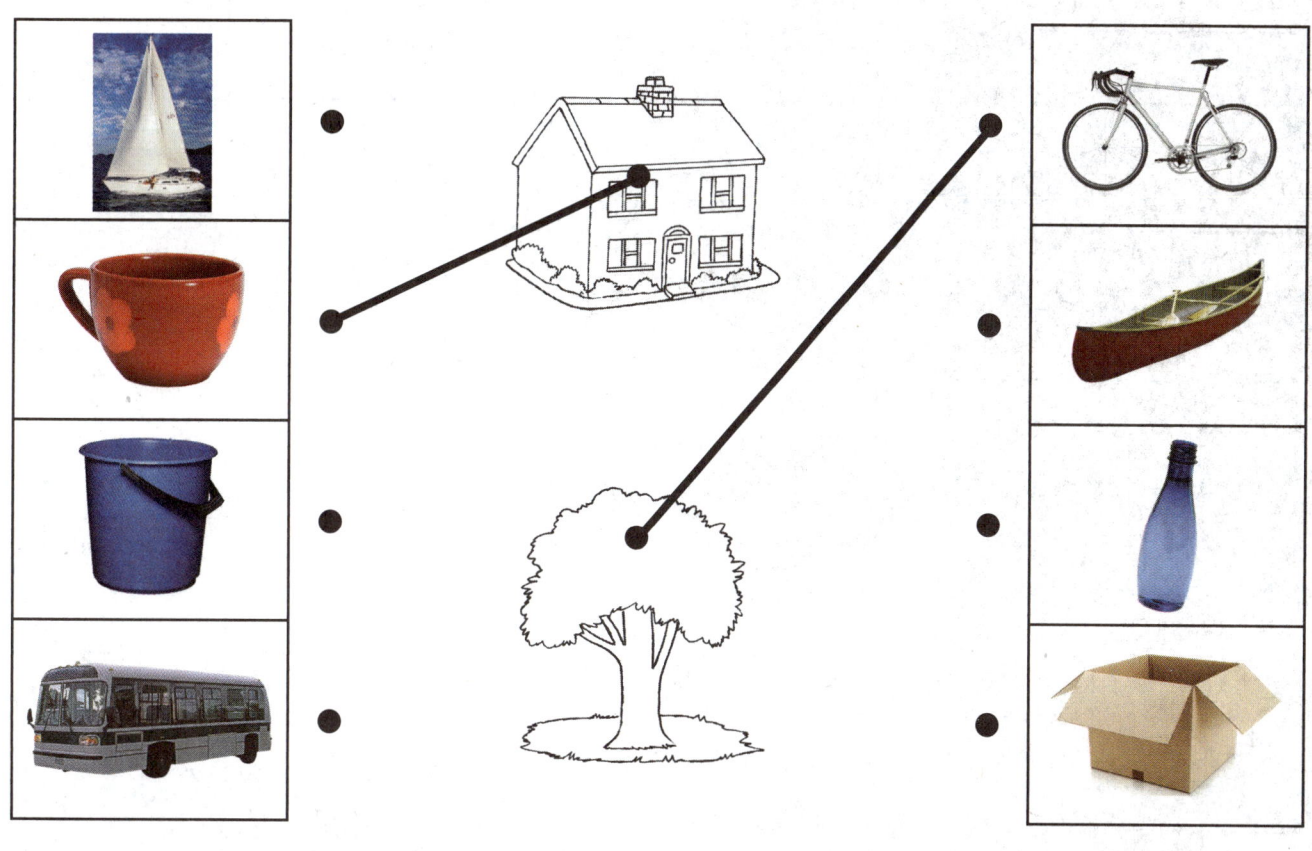

Side 1

Side 2

90

Side 1

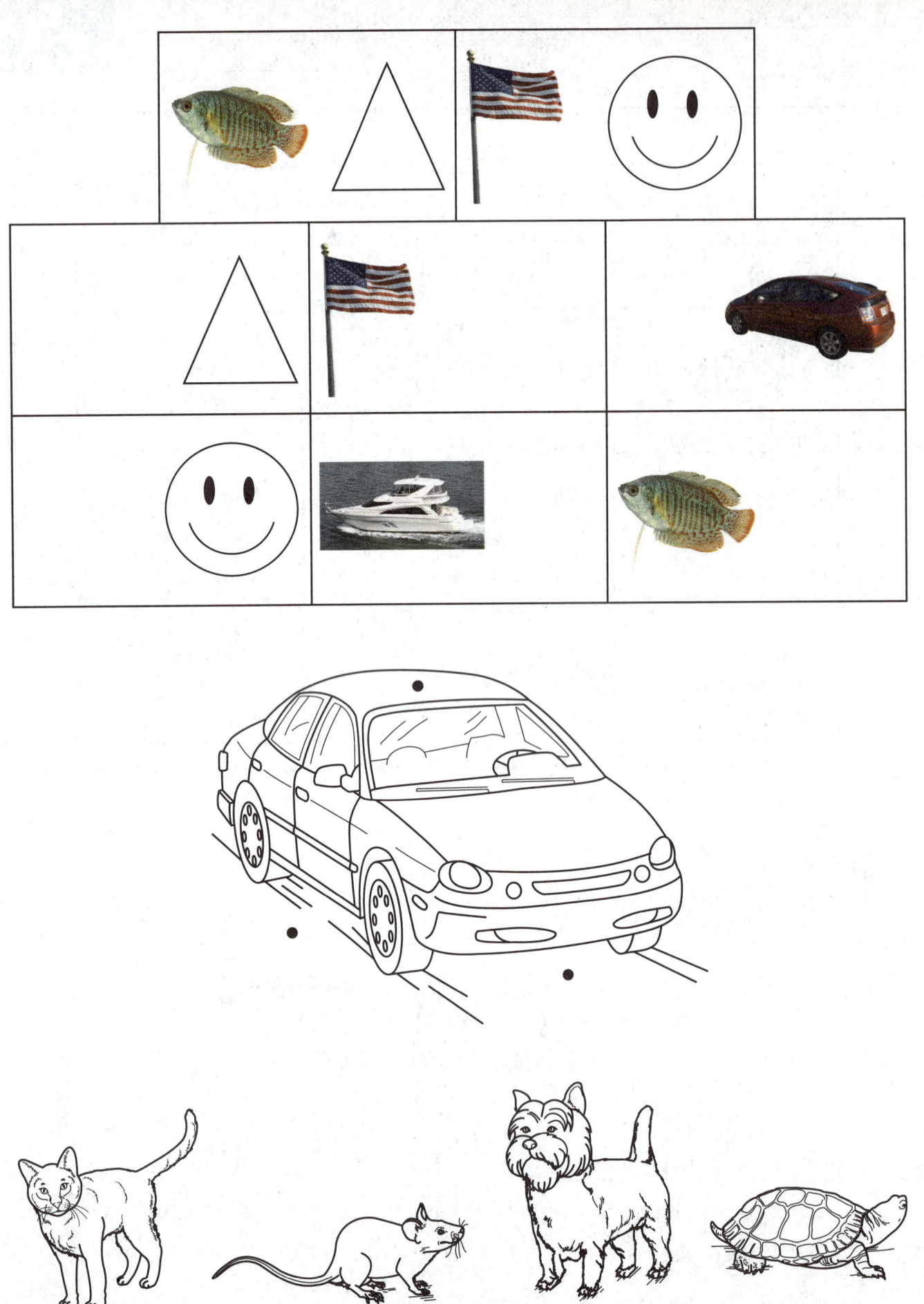

Side 2

_____
_ _
_____

| | pig | hen | lazy |
| chicks | busy | good | worked |

This story was about a little red
_____
_ _ _ _ _ _
_____ .

She _____ hard to make bread.

The other animals were too _____
to help her.

The hen shared the bread with her
_____
_ _ _ _ _ _
_____ .

This was a _____ story.

Side 1

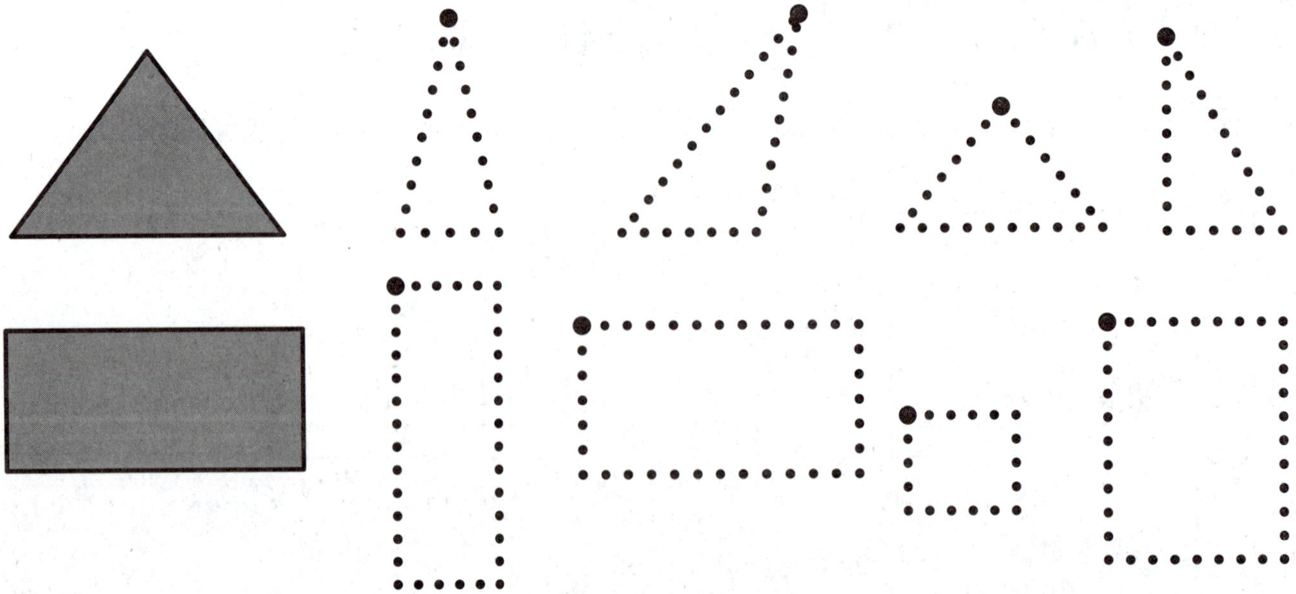

Side 2

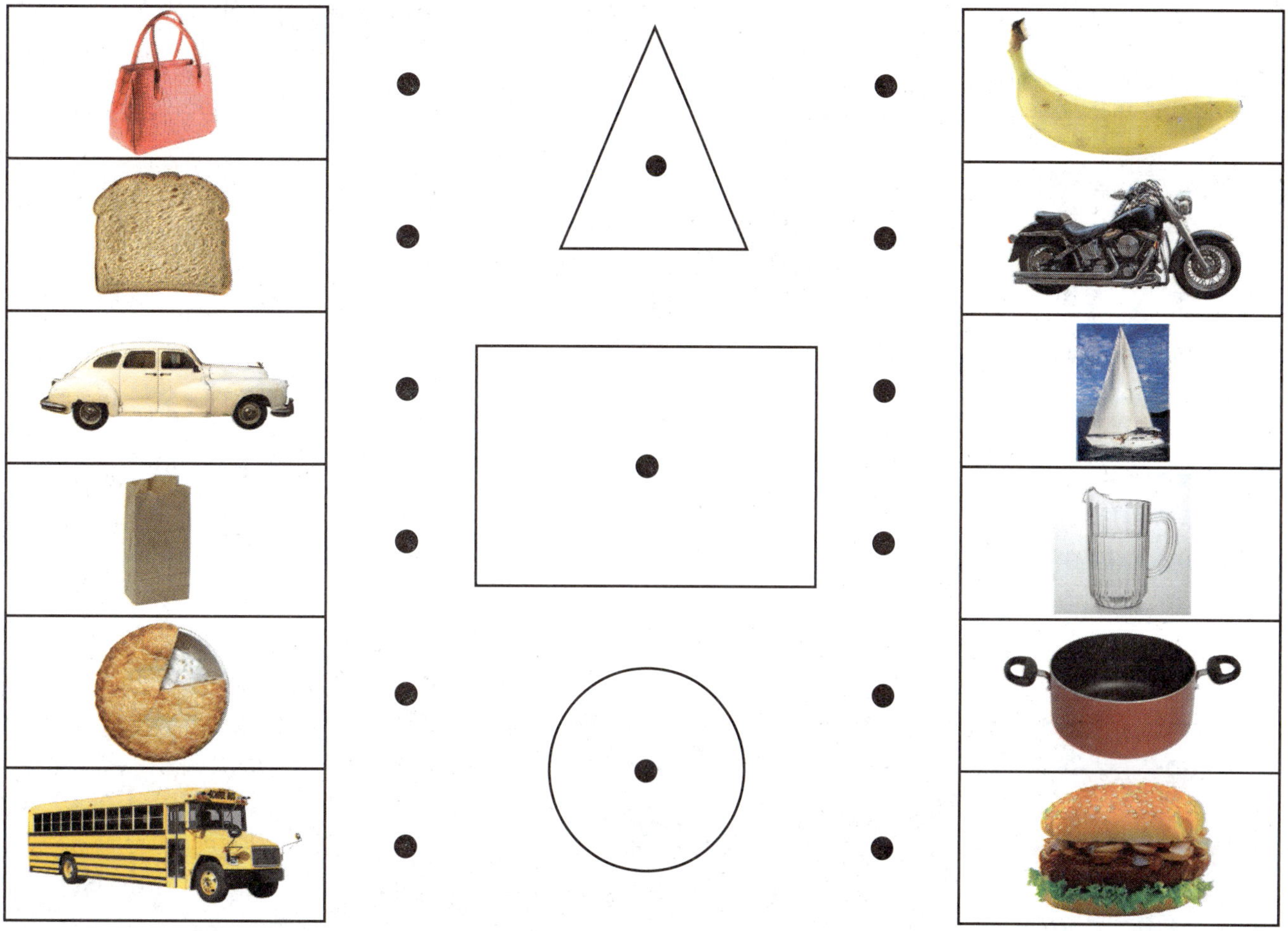

92

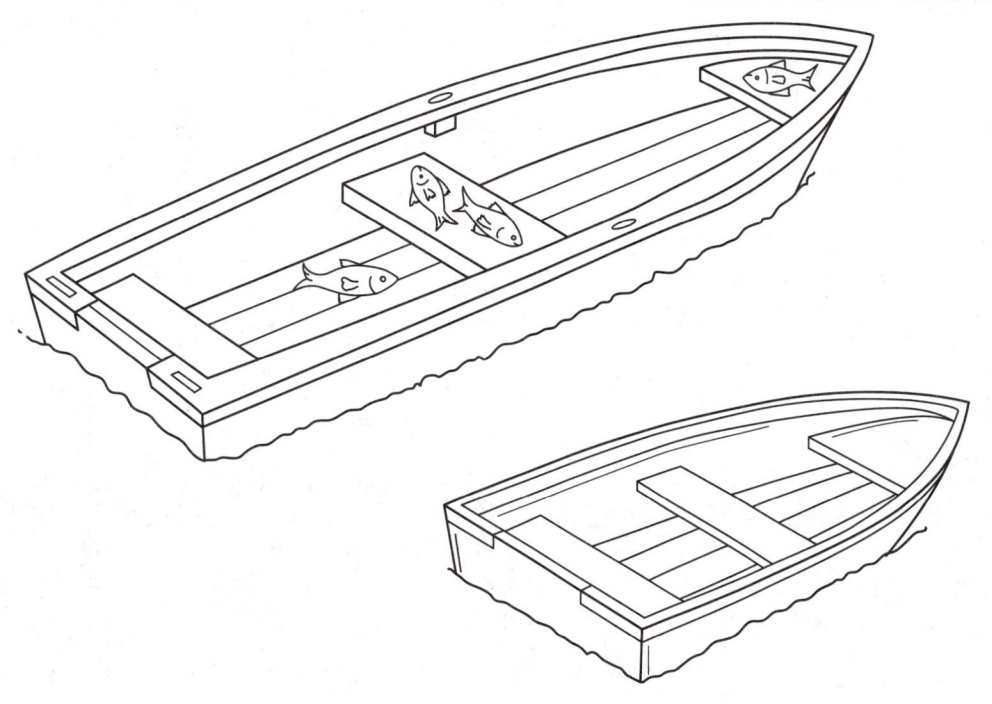

Side 1

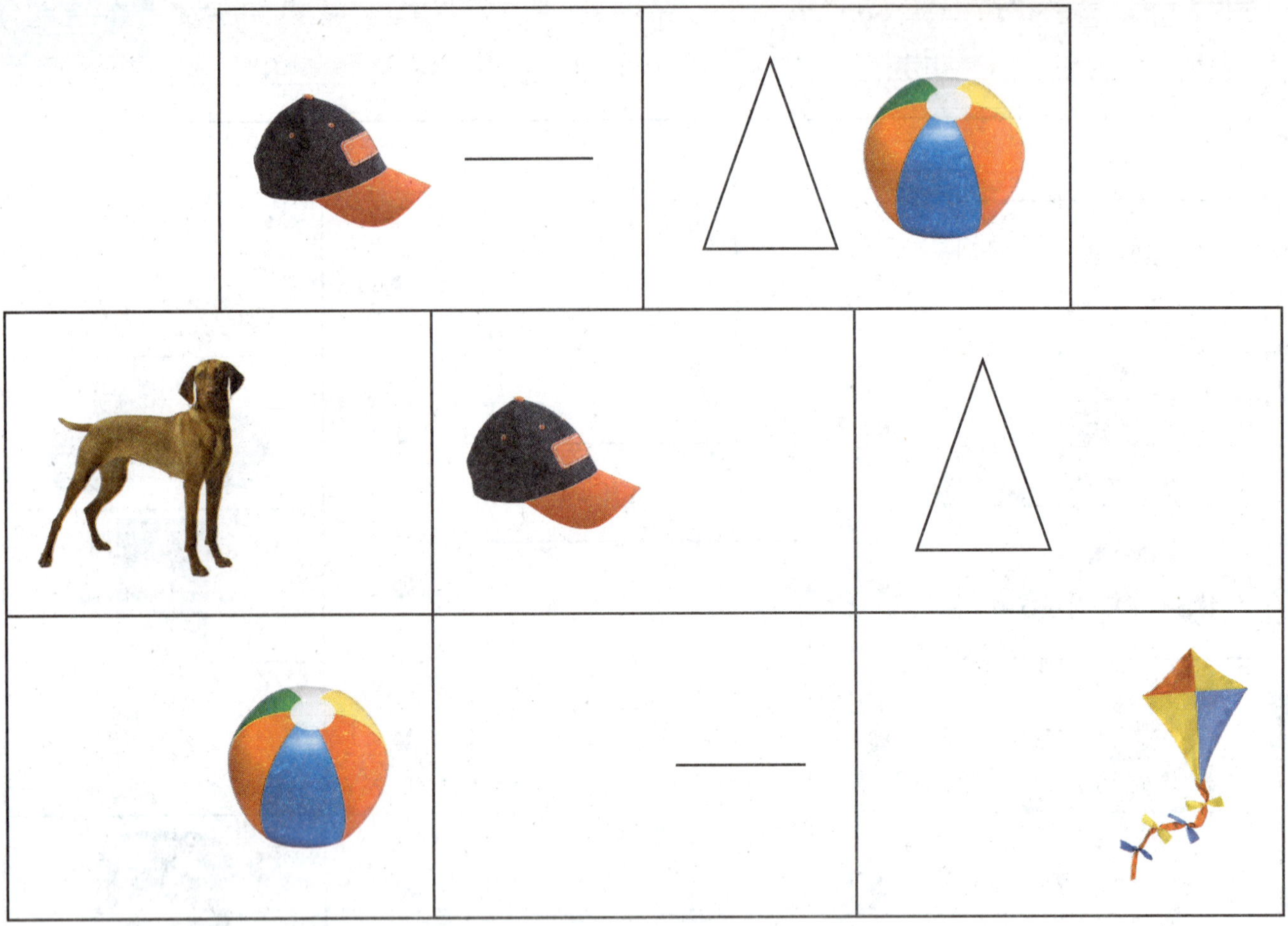

Side 2

93

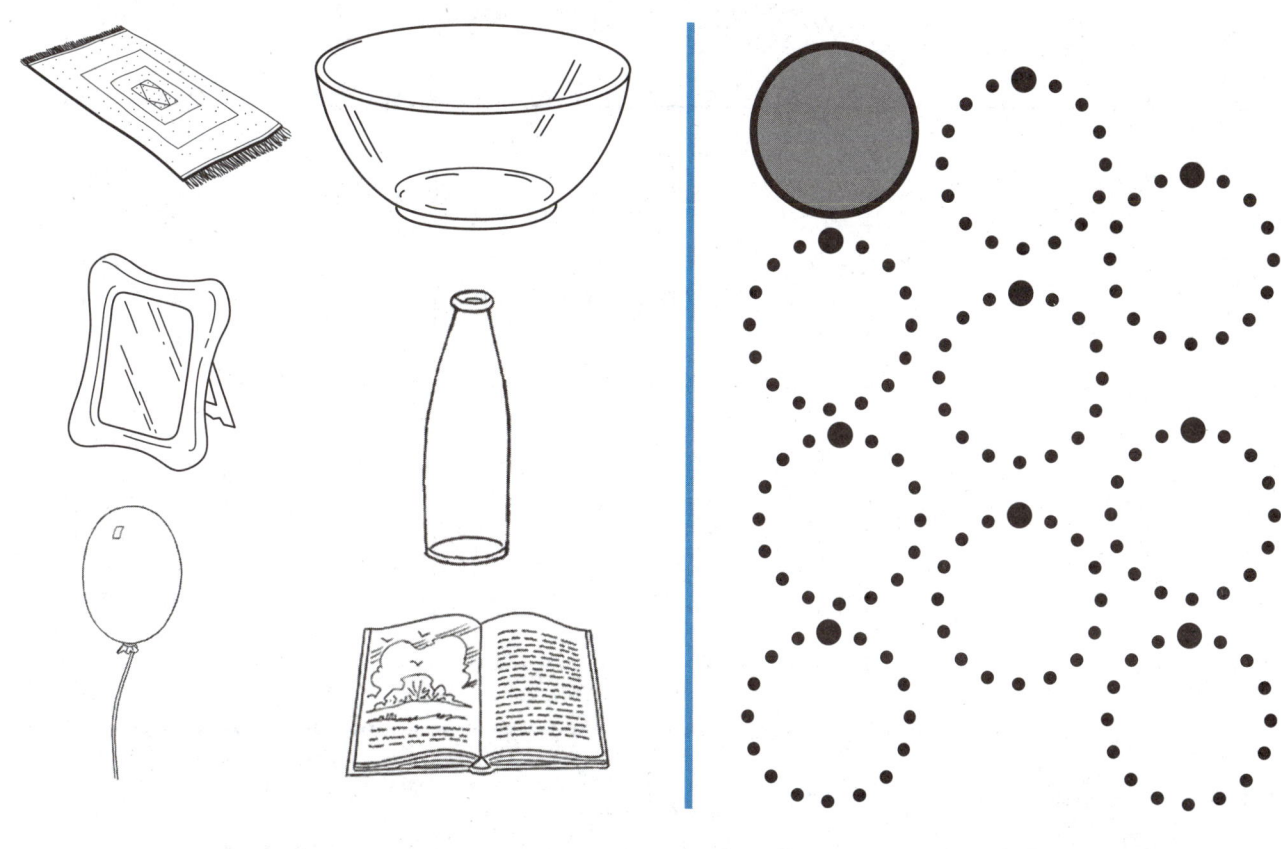

Side 1

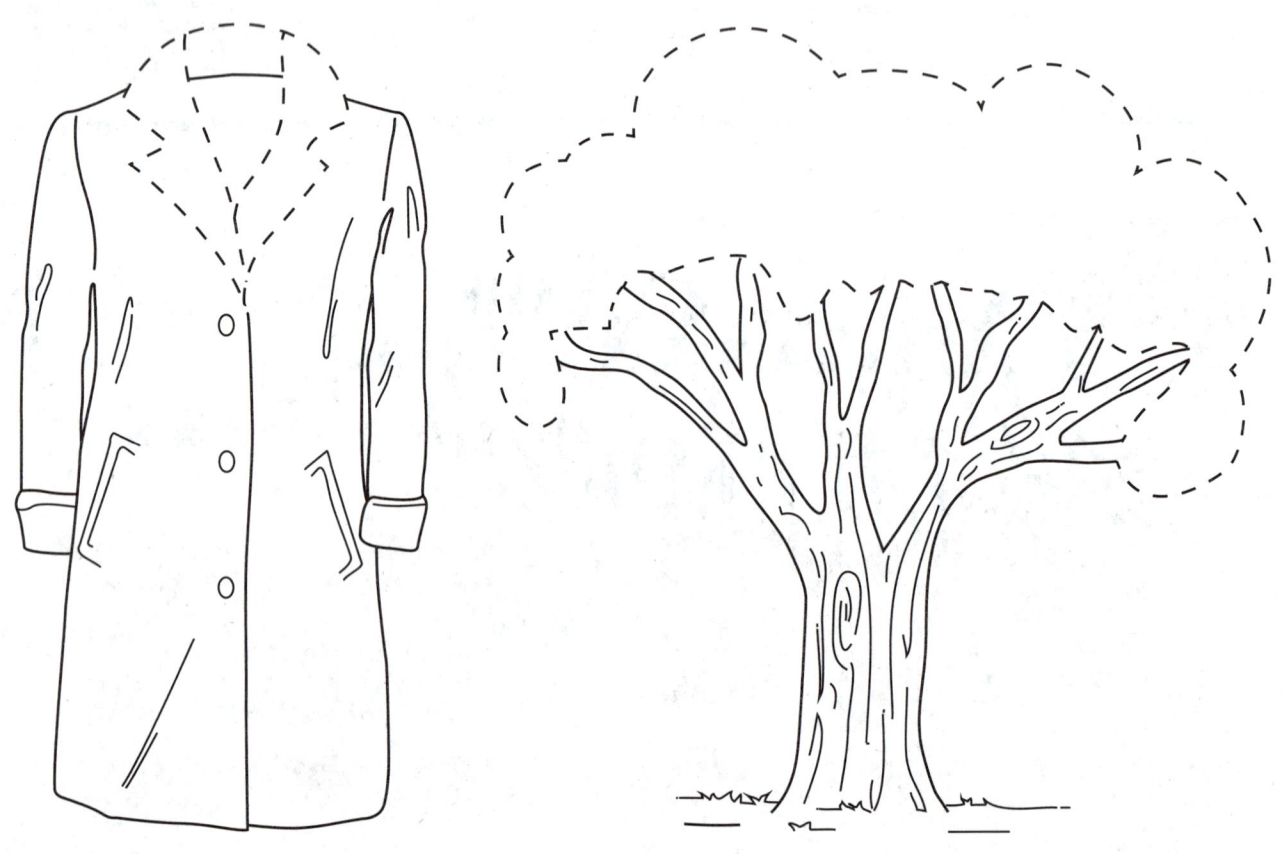

Side 2

94

Side 1

Side 2

Side 1

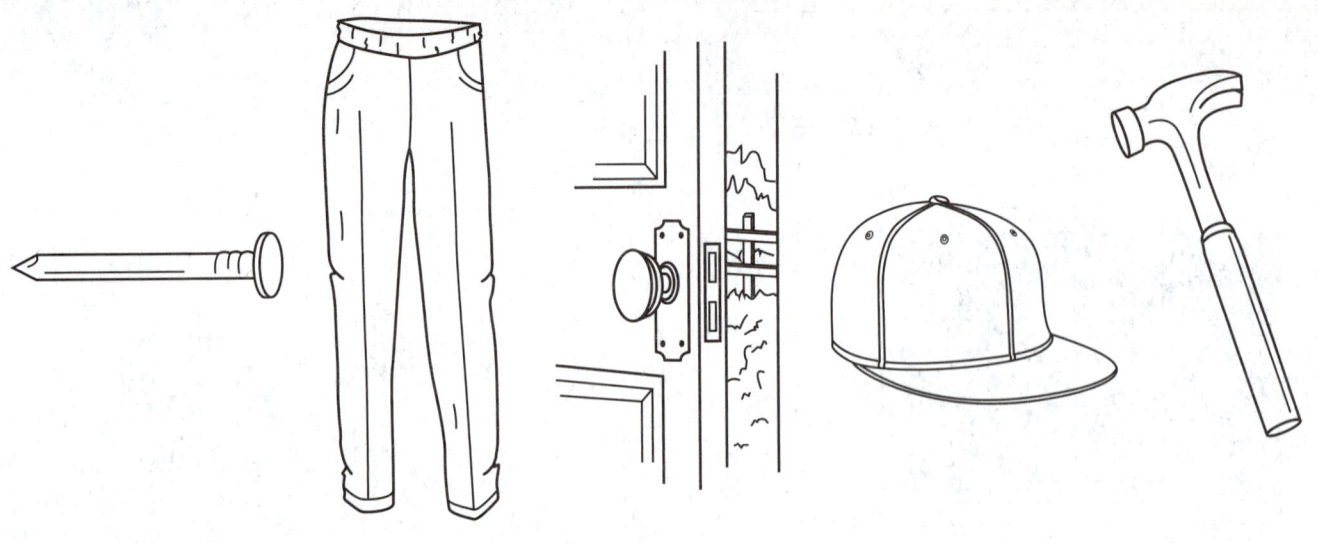

Side 2

eagle   pig   bread
real   wire   paint   happy

Paul spilled _____ on the porch.

Clarabelle jumped off a _____ .

Sweetie was scared by an _____ .

Timmy's rabbit turned into a _____ rabbit.

The little red hen made _____ by herself.

Side 2

97

The color I like most is _____.

Side 1

Side 2

98

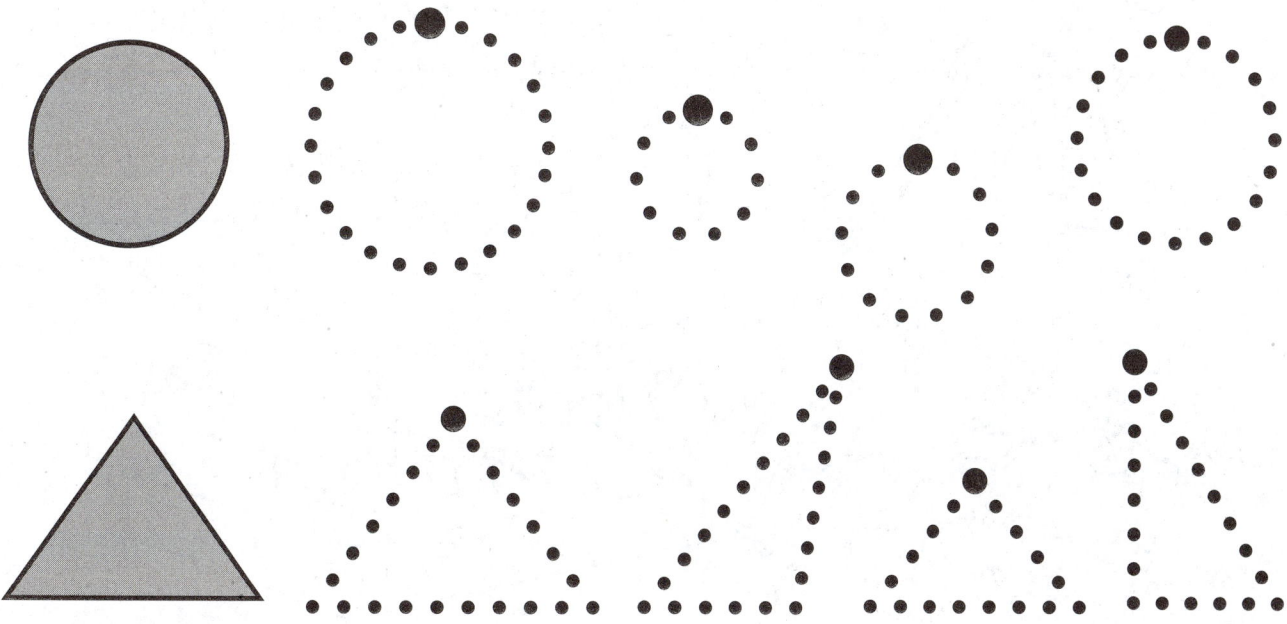

Side 1

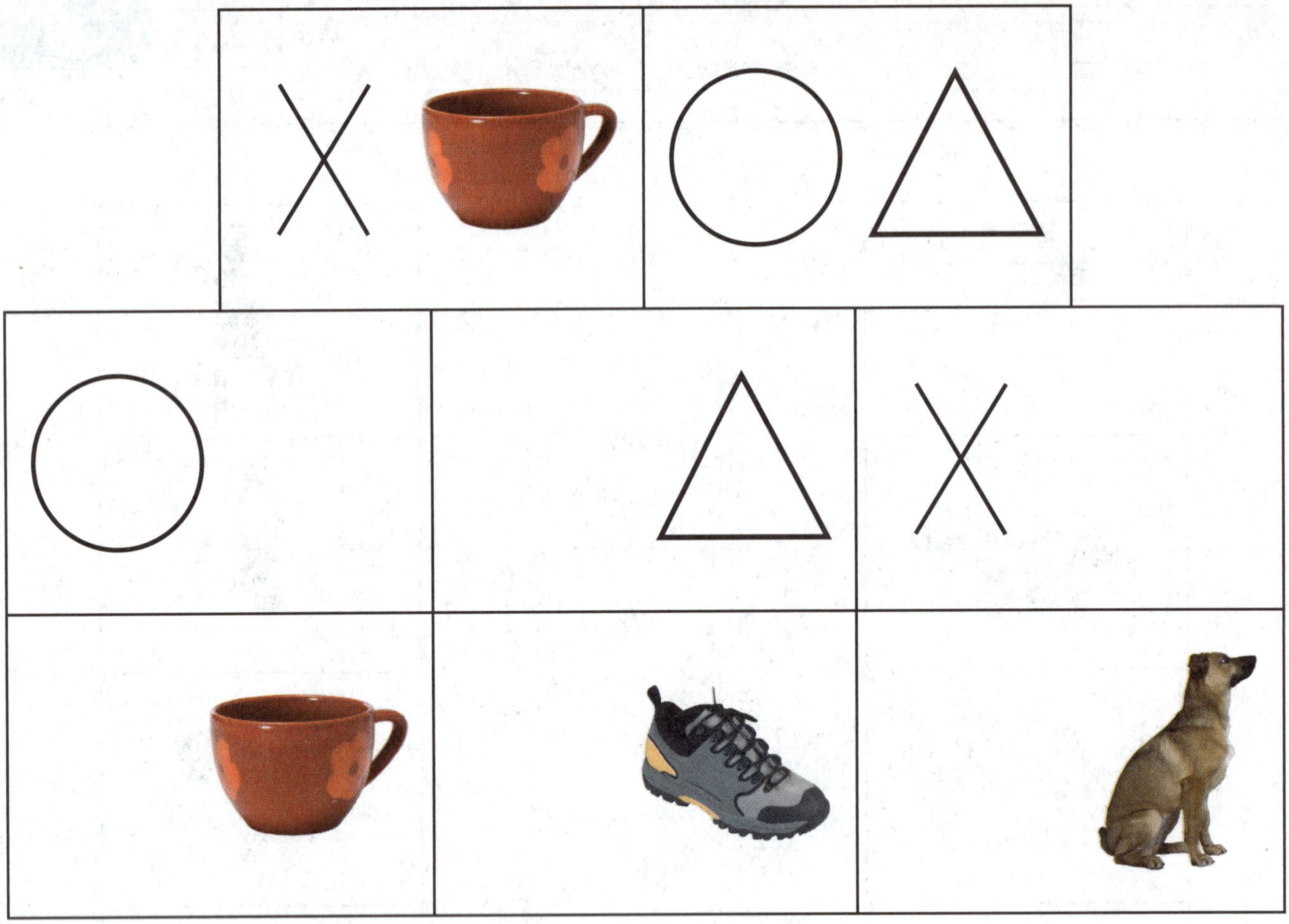

Side 2

The vehicle I like most is a _____.

I would like to travel to the _____.

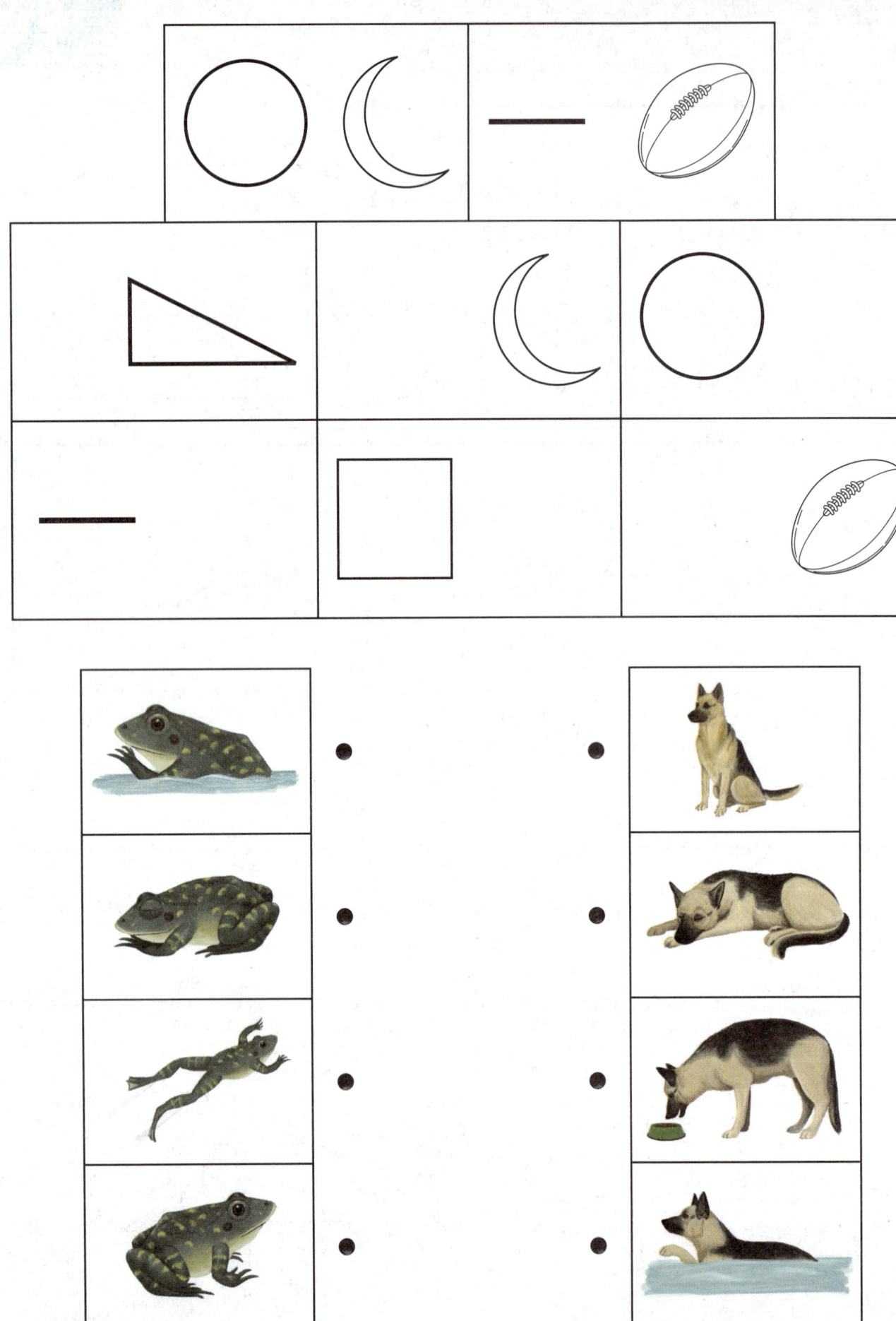

Side 2

100

Side 1

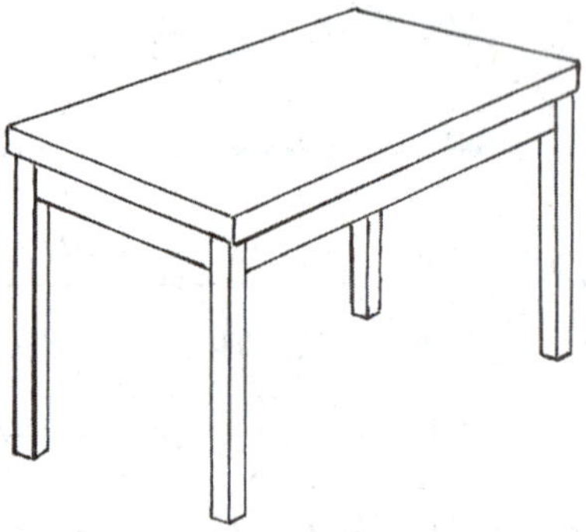

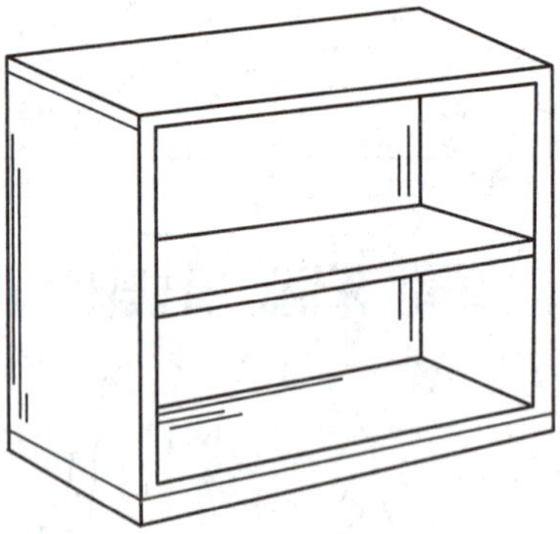

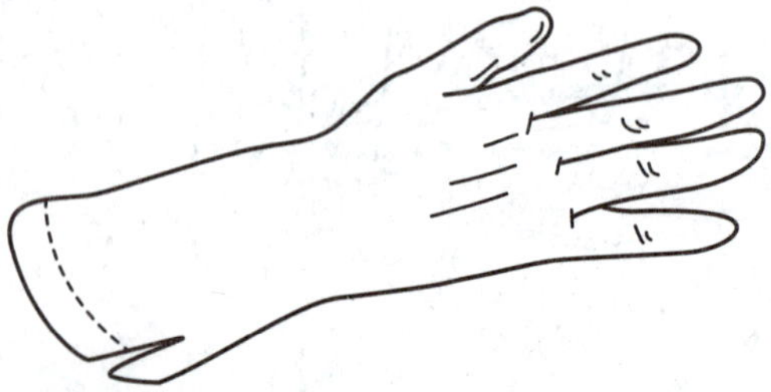

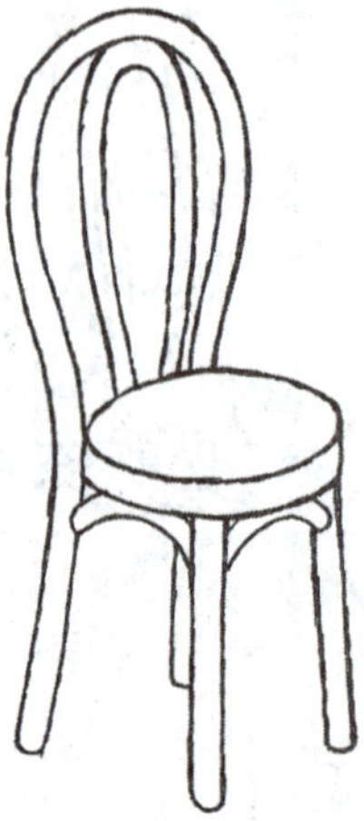

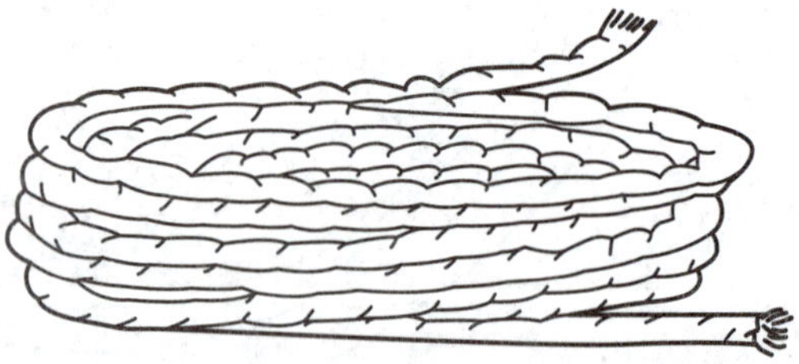

Side 2

_____
_____

ant	spider	eyes	bee	
	legs	centipede	butterfly	

Lots of bugs have 6 _____ .

A _____ has 6 legs and makes honey.

A _____ has 8 legs.

A _____ has 100 legs or more.

Side 1

Side 2

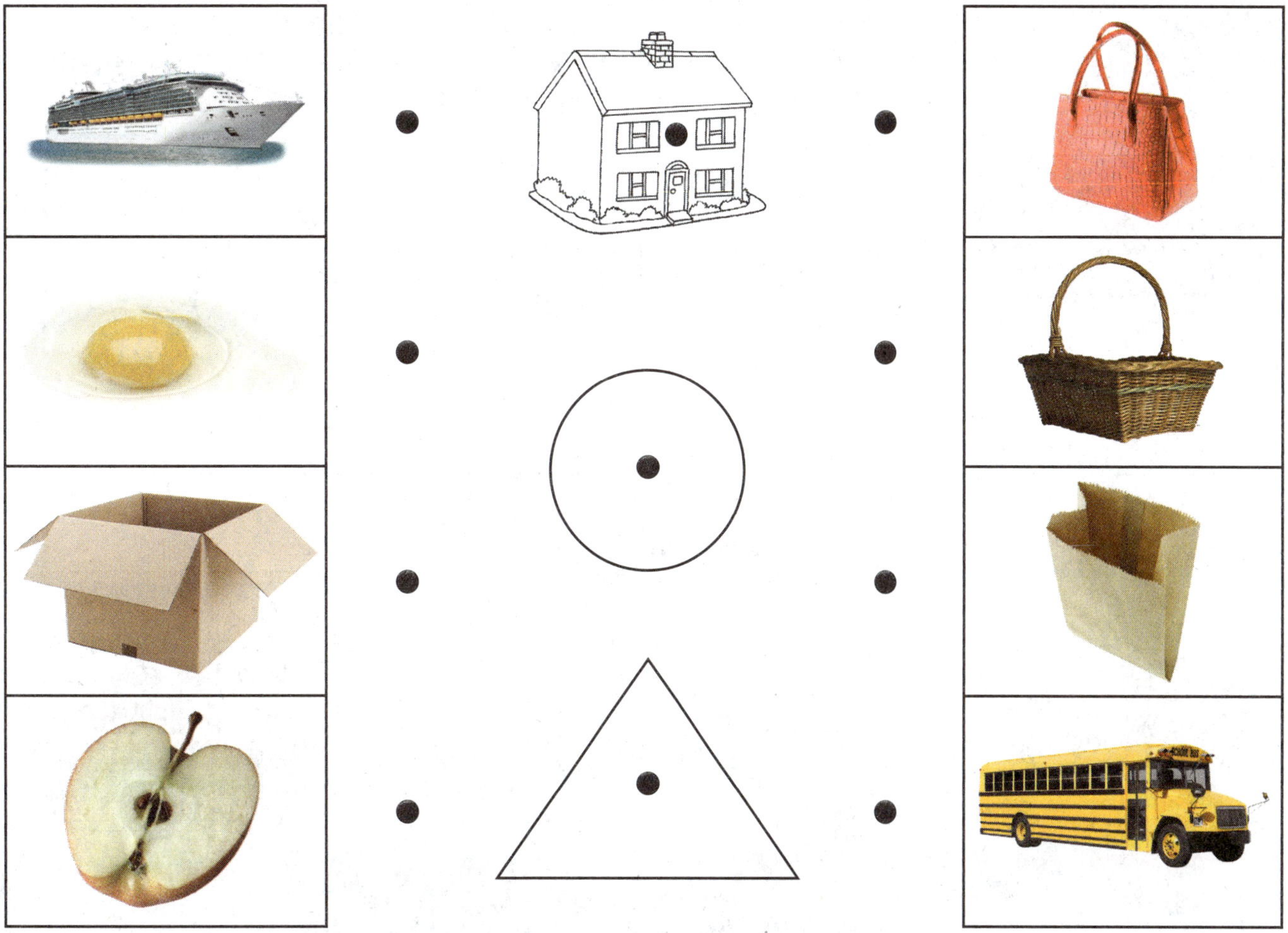

102

Side 1

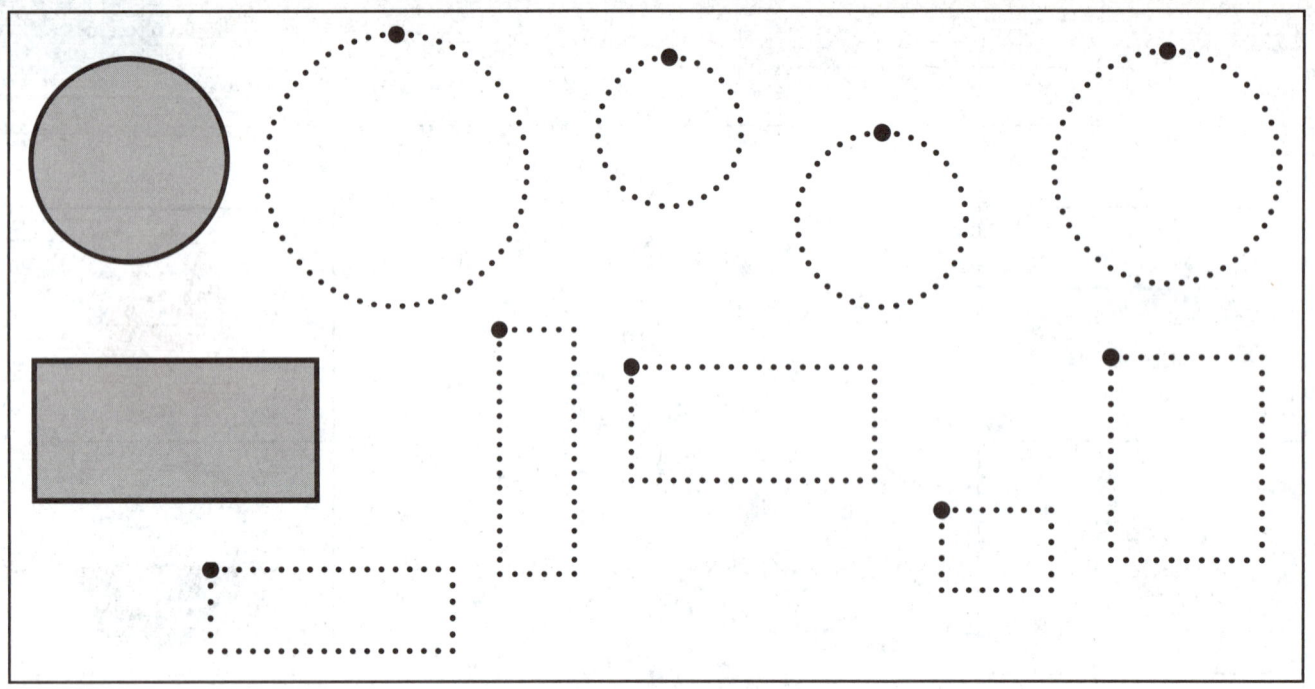

Side 2

103

Side 1

Side 2

104

Side 1

Side 2

105

Side 1

| mouse | happy | promise | good |
| friends | thorn | funny | |

The mouse made a _____ to help the lion.

The lion had a _____ in his paw.

The _____ pulled the thorn out of his paw.

The lion and the mouse became great _____.

This was a _____ story.

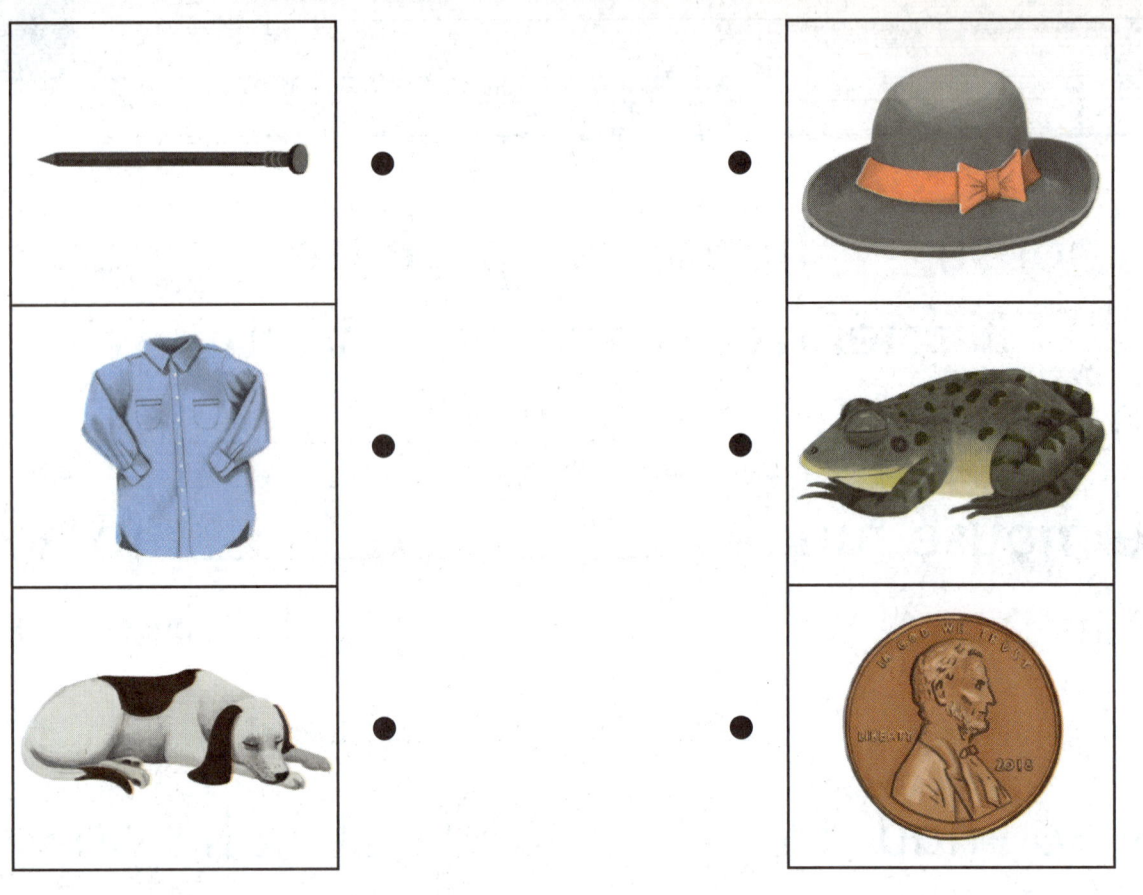

Side 2

107

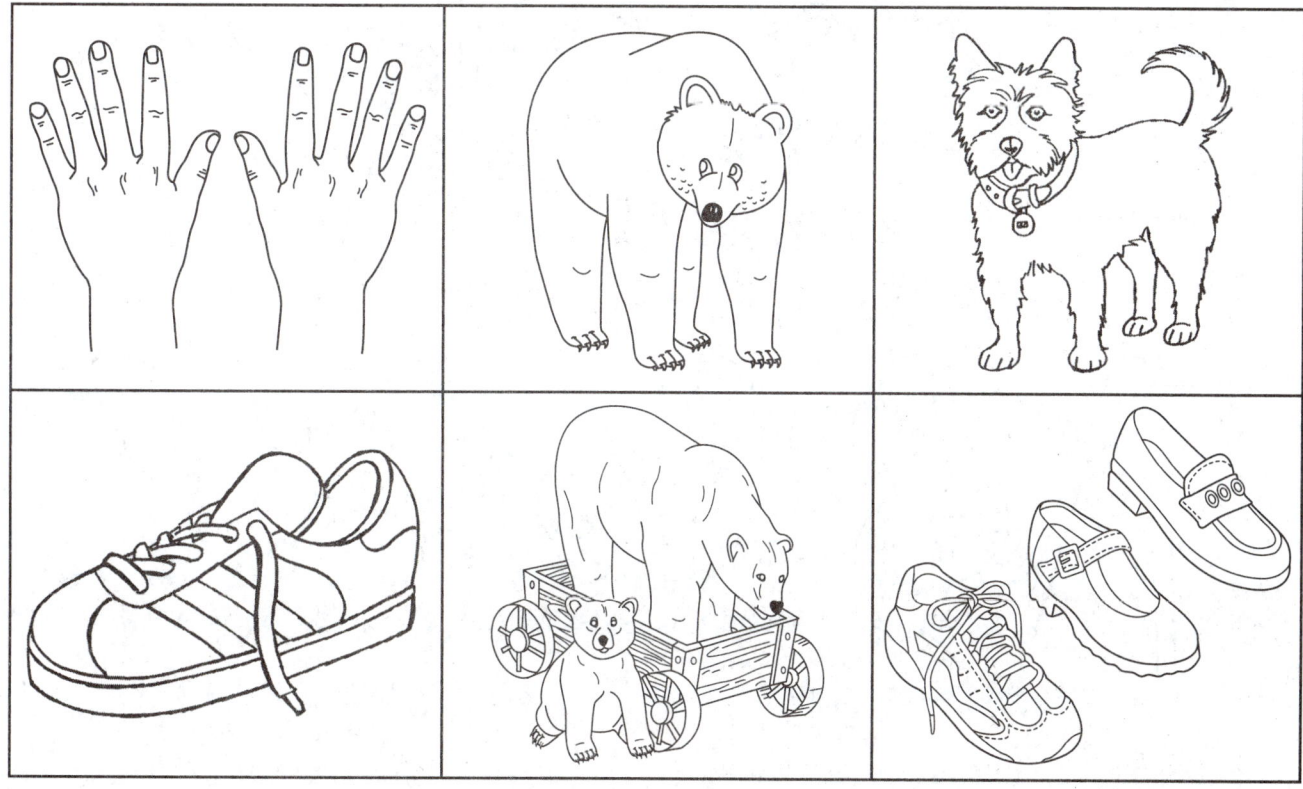

Side 1

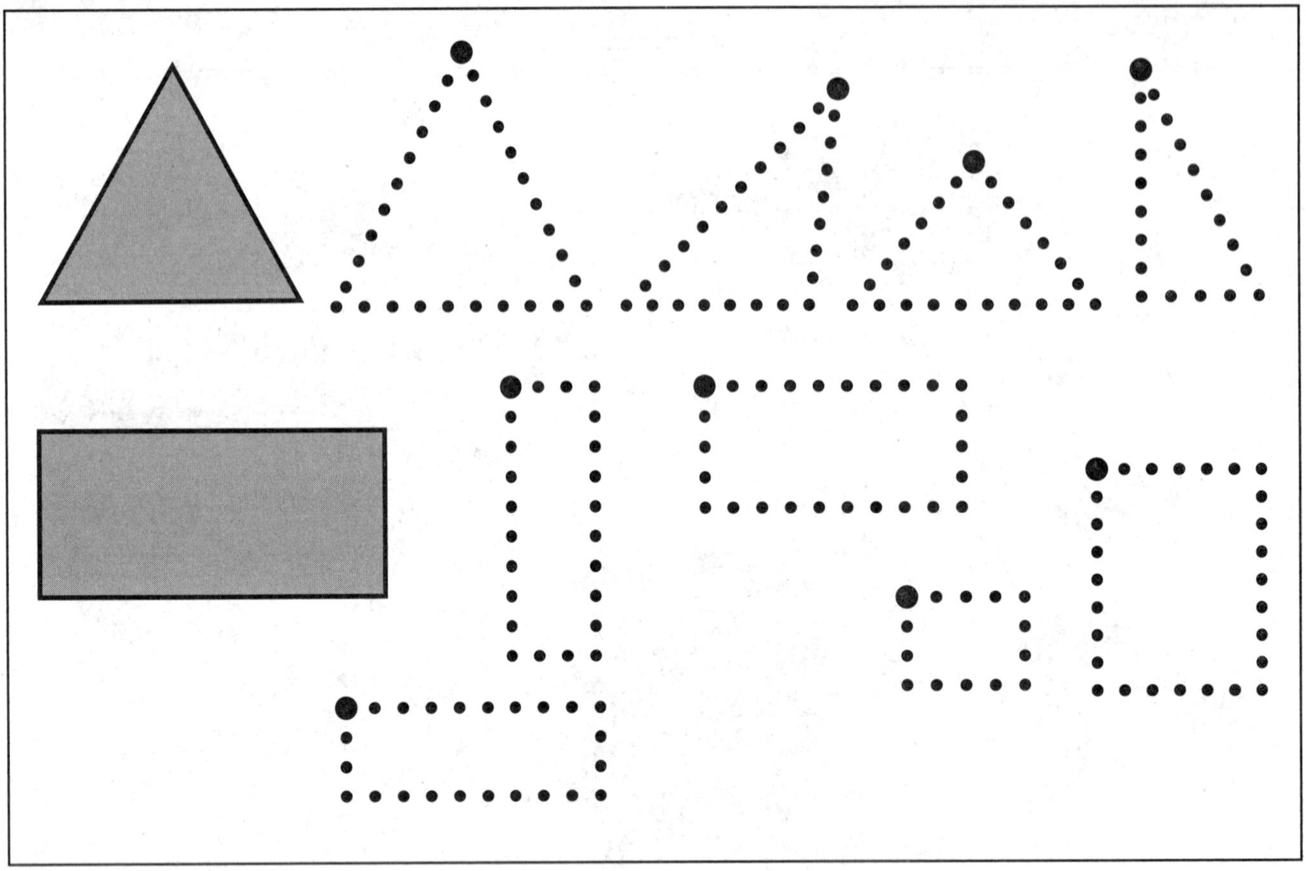

Side 2

108

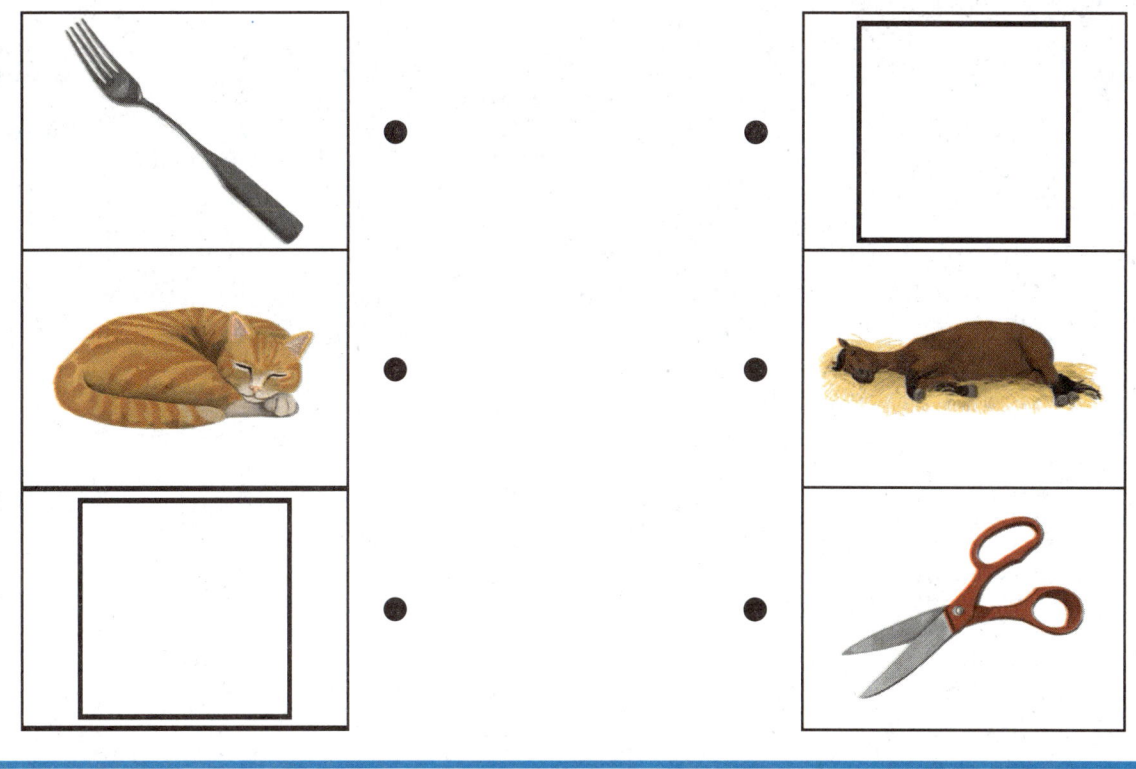

Side 1

Side 2

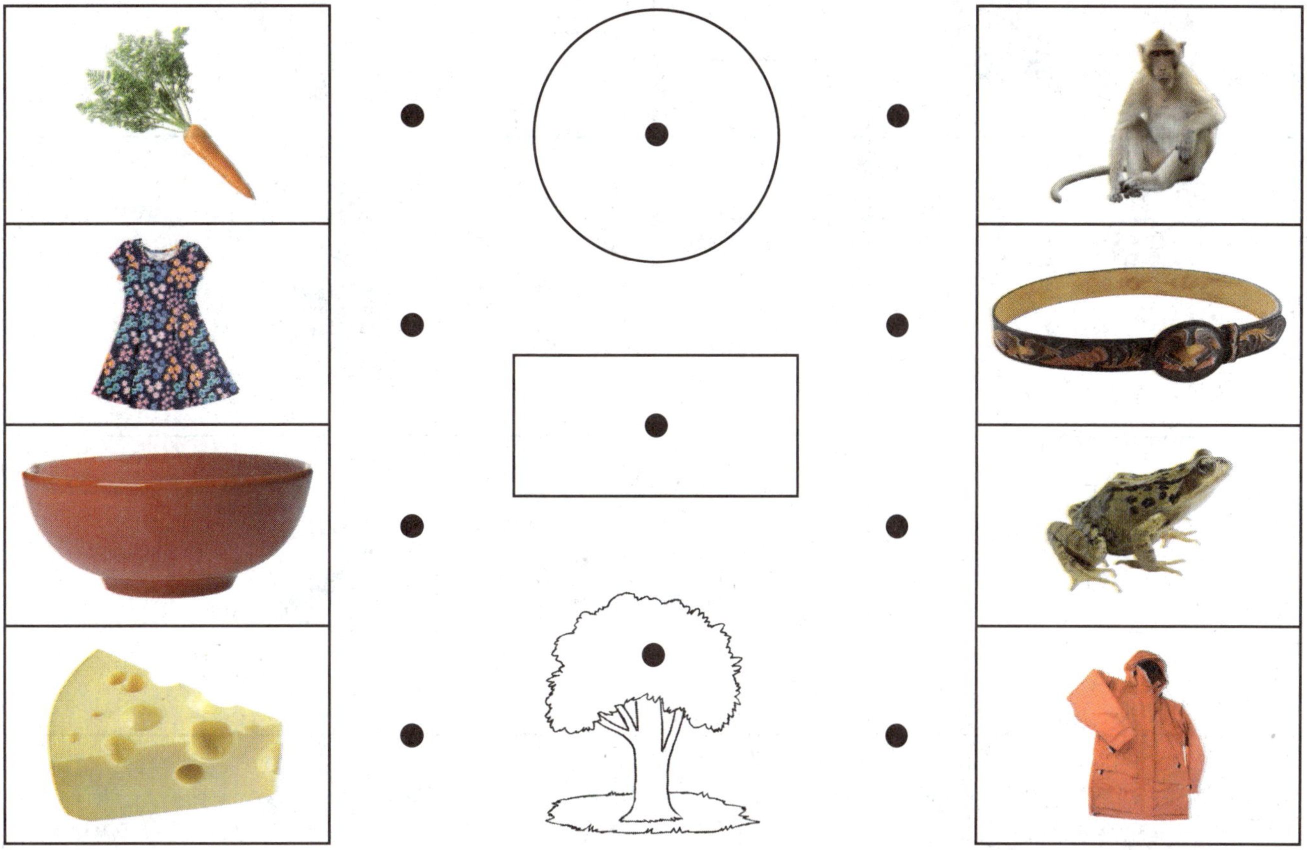

109

Side 1

Side 2

110

Side 1

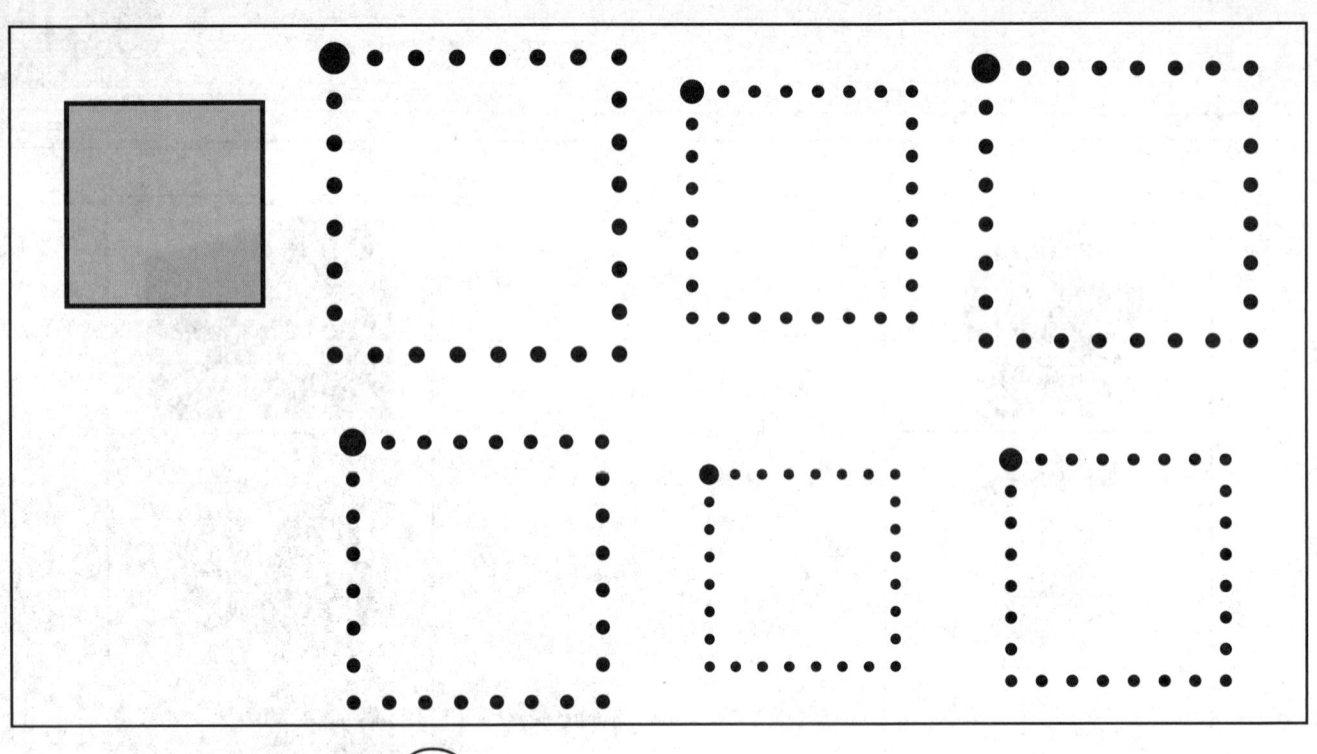

Side 2

pupa   legs   life
adult   egg   bug   larva

This book is about the _____ cycle of a butterfly.

A butterfly starts out as a tiny _____.

The butterfly turns into a _____ after it is born.

Then the butterfly grows inside a _____.

The picture shows an _____ butterfly.

Side 1

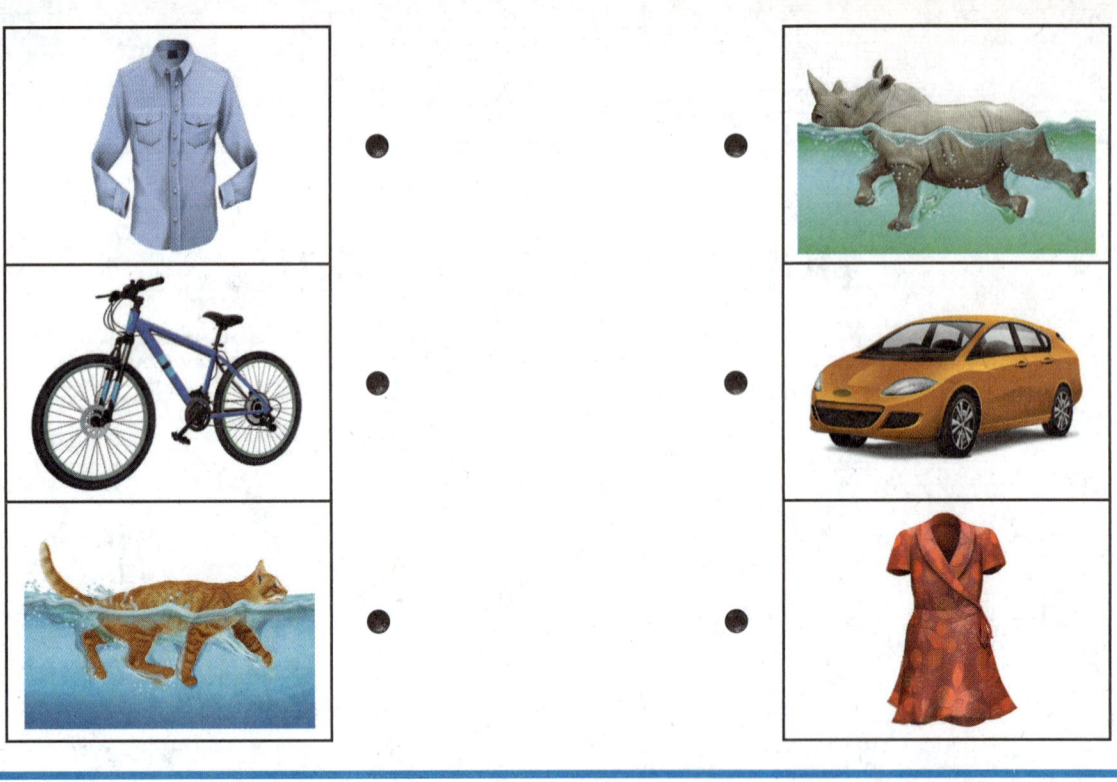

Side 2

112

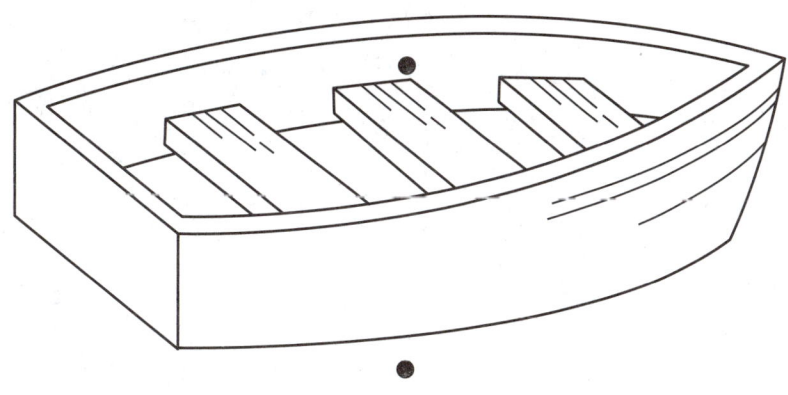

Side 1

113

Side 1

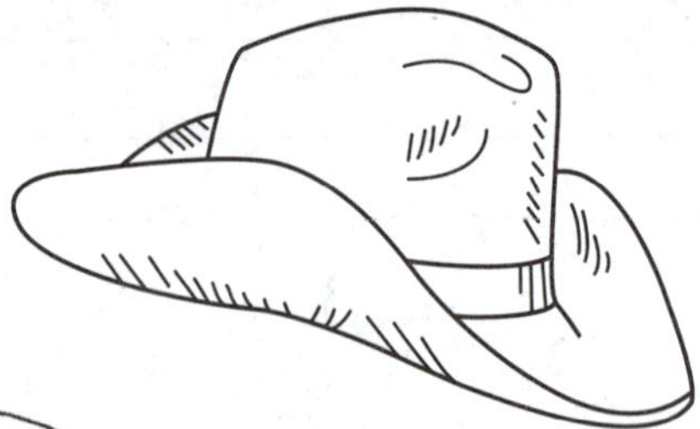

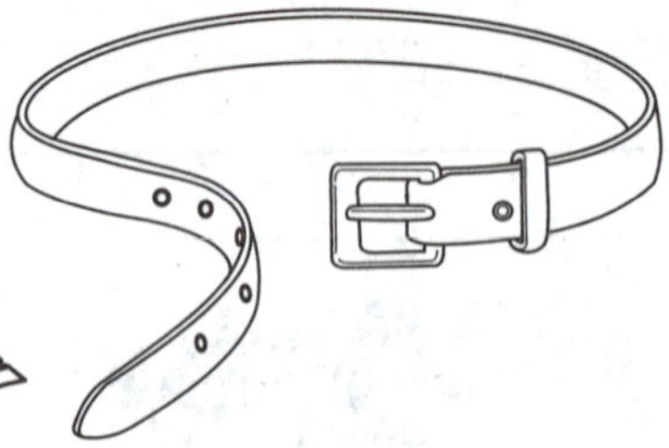

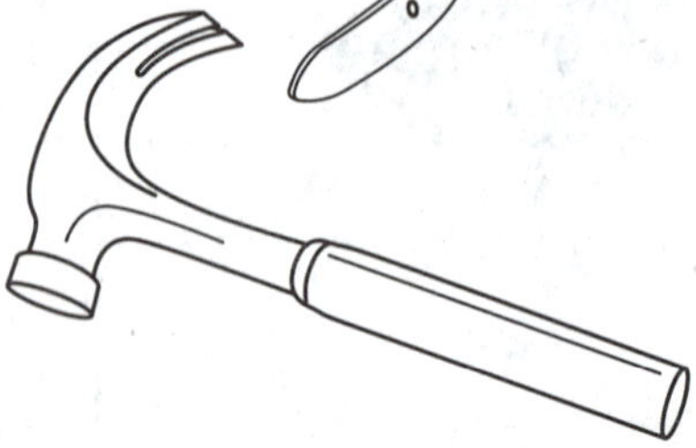

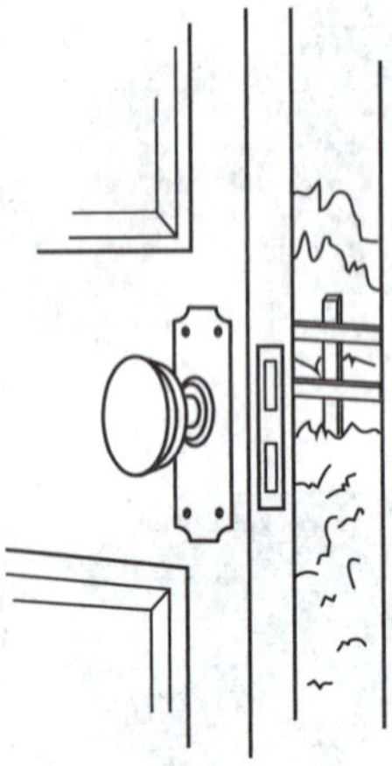

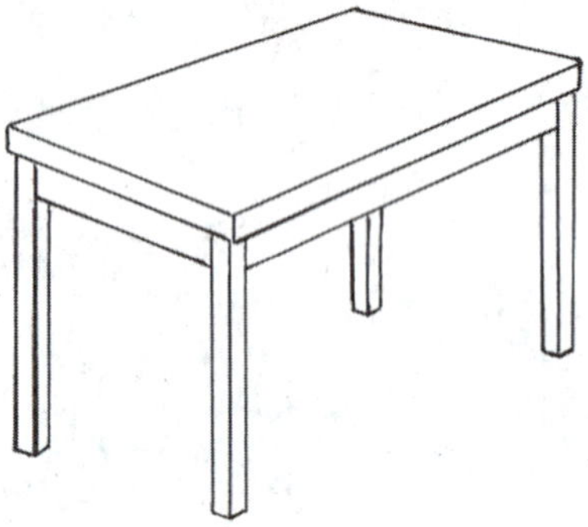

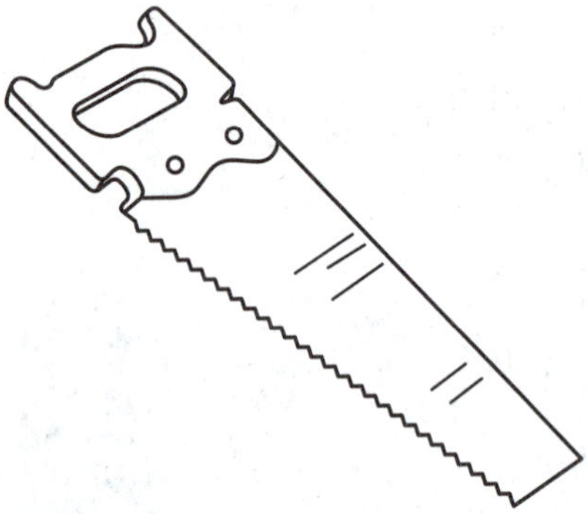

Side 2

Side 1

Side 2

115

Side 1

Side 2

116

Side 1

Side 2

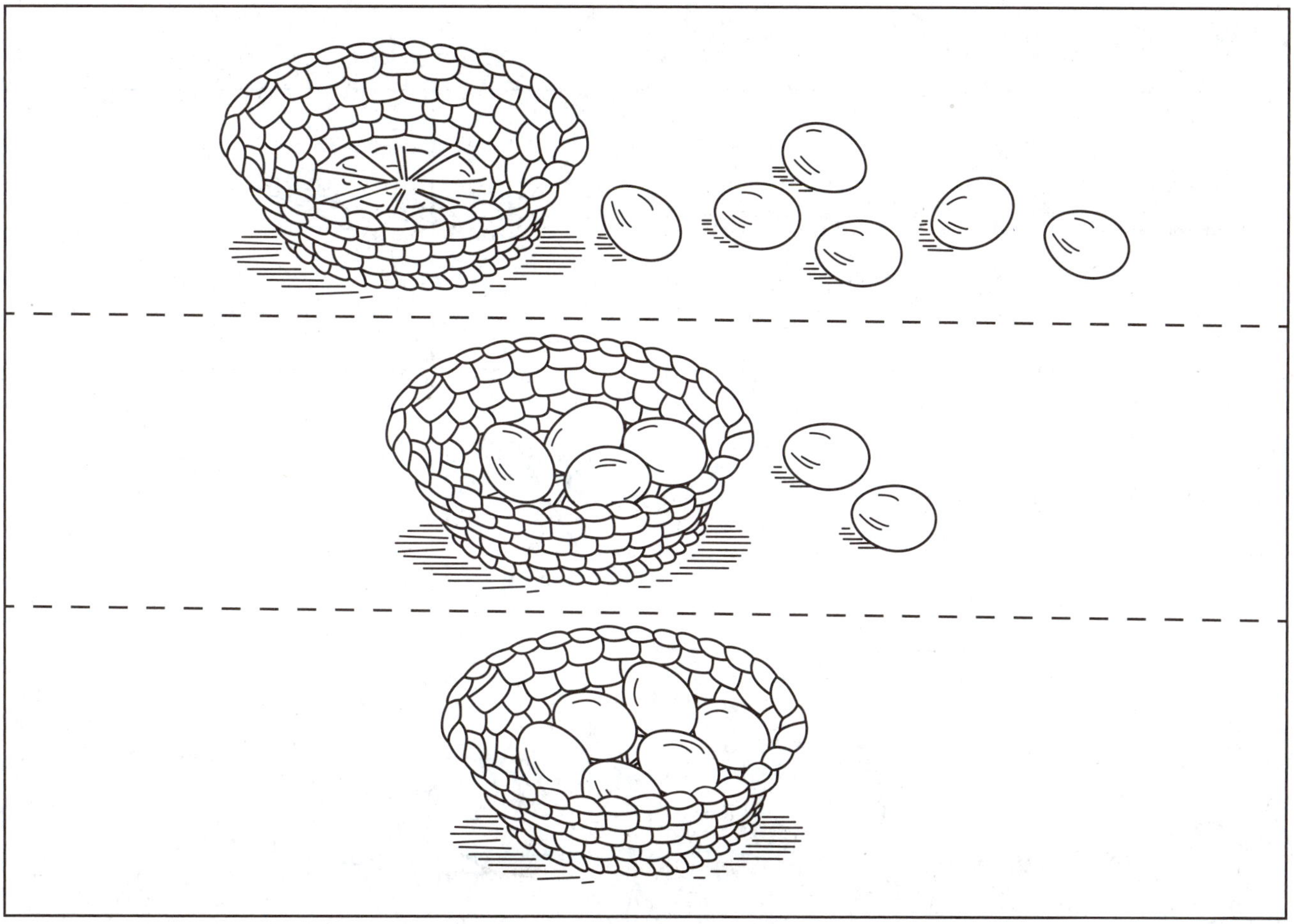

117

Side 1

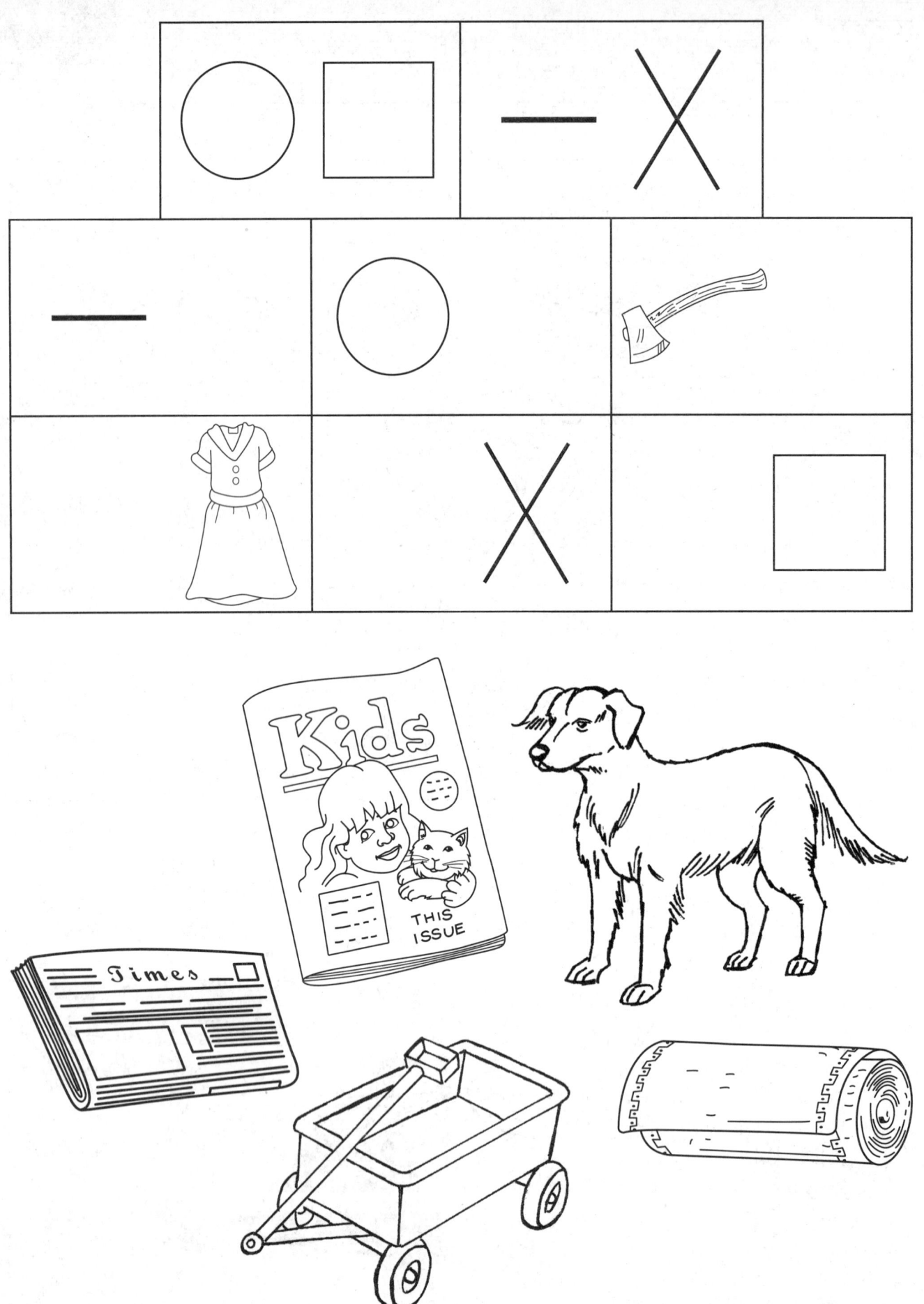

Side 2

118

Side 1

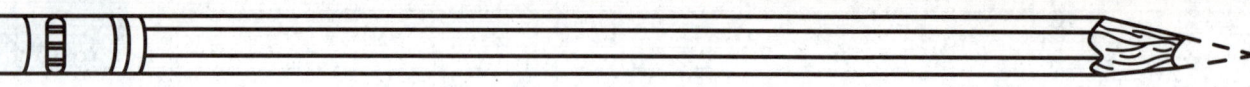

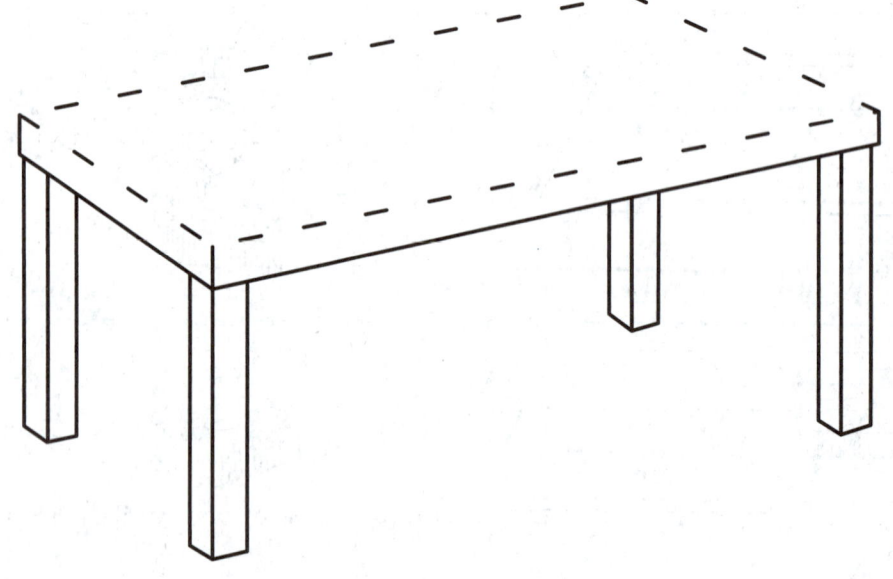

Side 2

Side 1

Side 2

120

Side 1

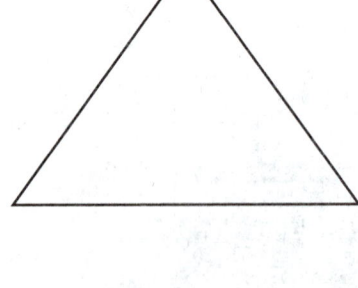 _____

 _____

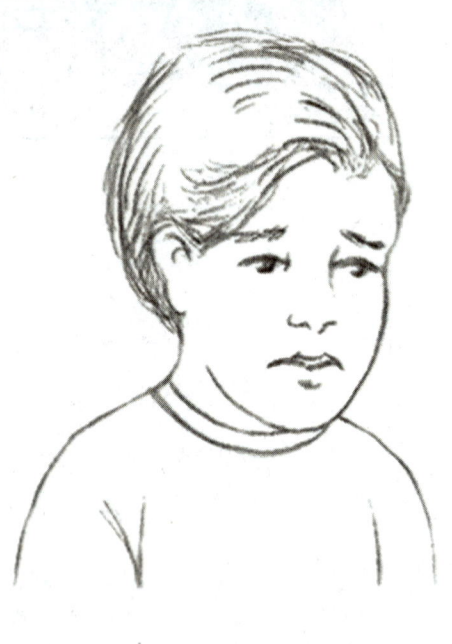

Side 2

| sun | warm | cold |
| same | moon | food | different |

Butterflies only fly when the _____ is out.

Butterflies migrate when it gets too _____.

One reason butterflies migrate is to stay _____.

Butterflies also migrate to find _____.

Butterflies always migrate to the _____ place.

Side 2

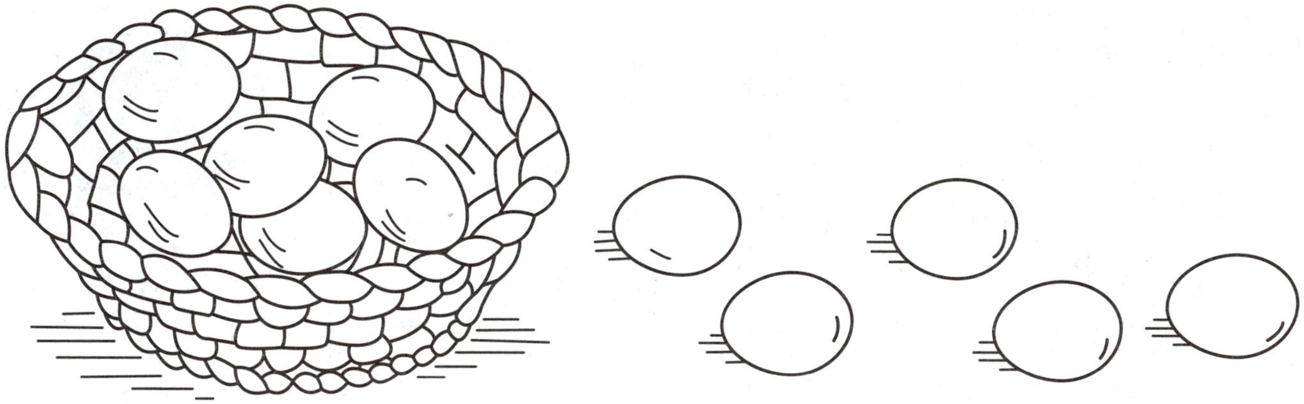

122

Side 1

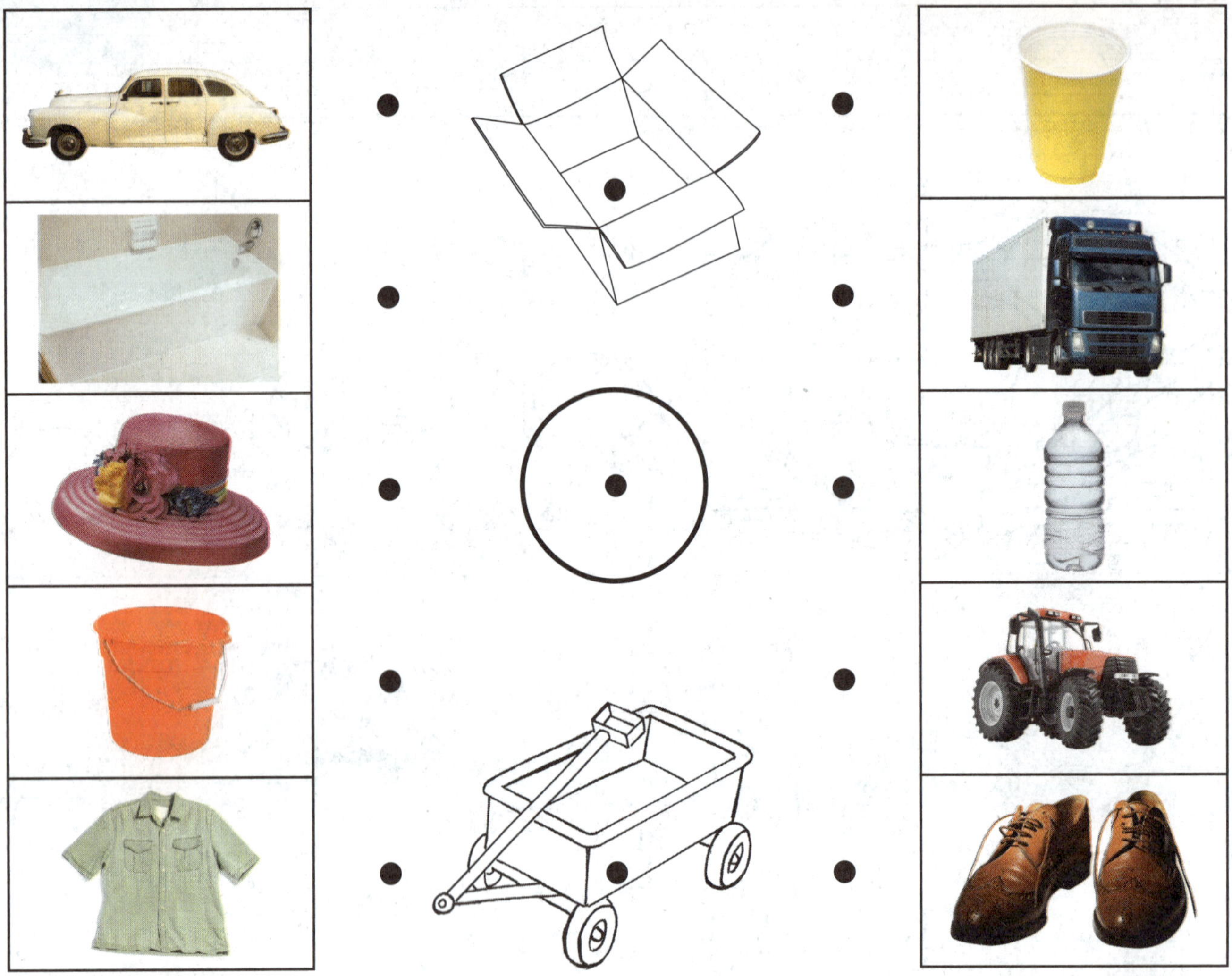

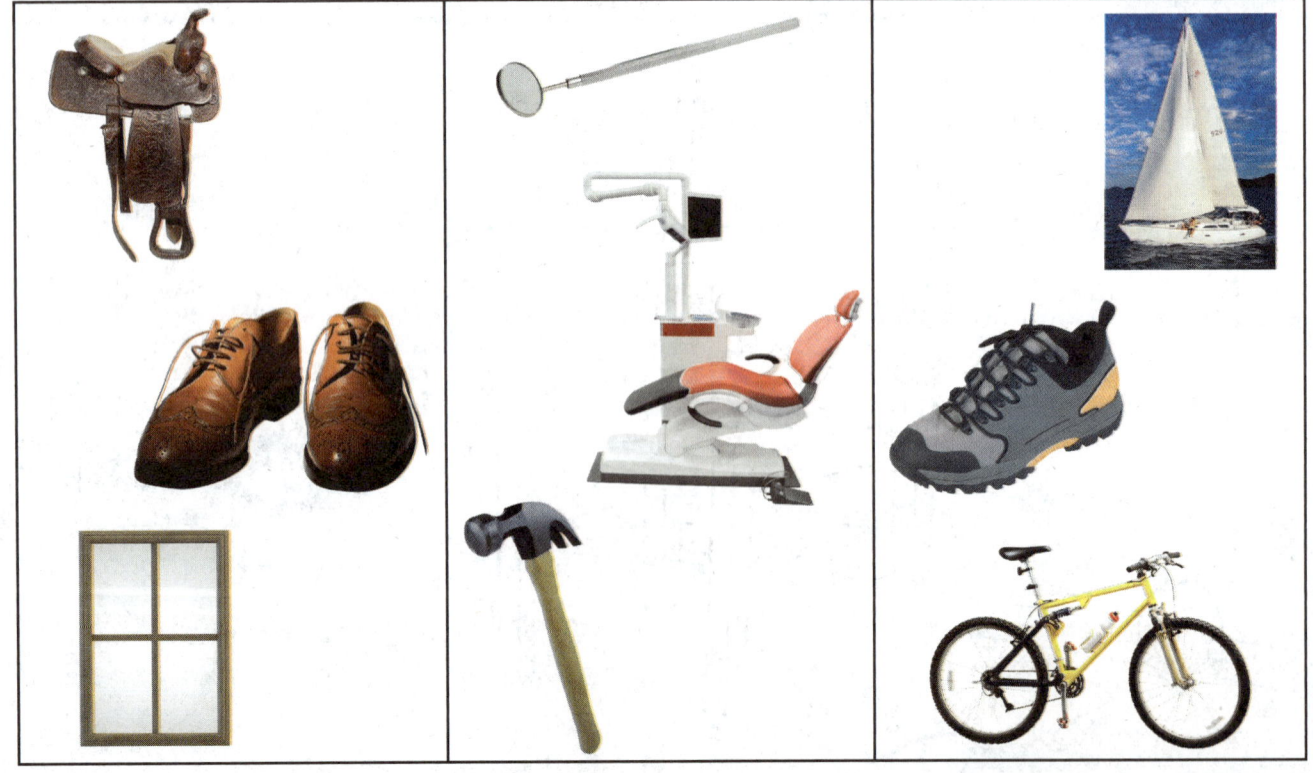

Side 2

123

Side 1

Side 2

124

Side 1

Side 2

125

Side 1

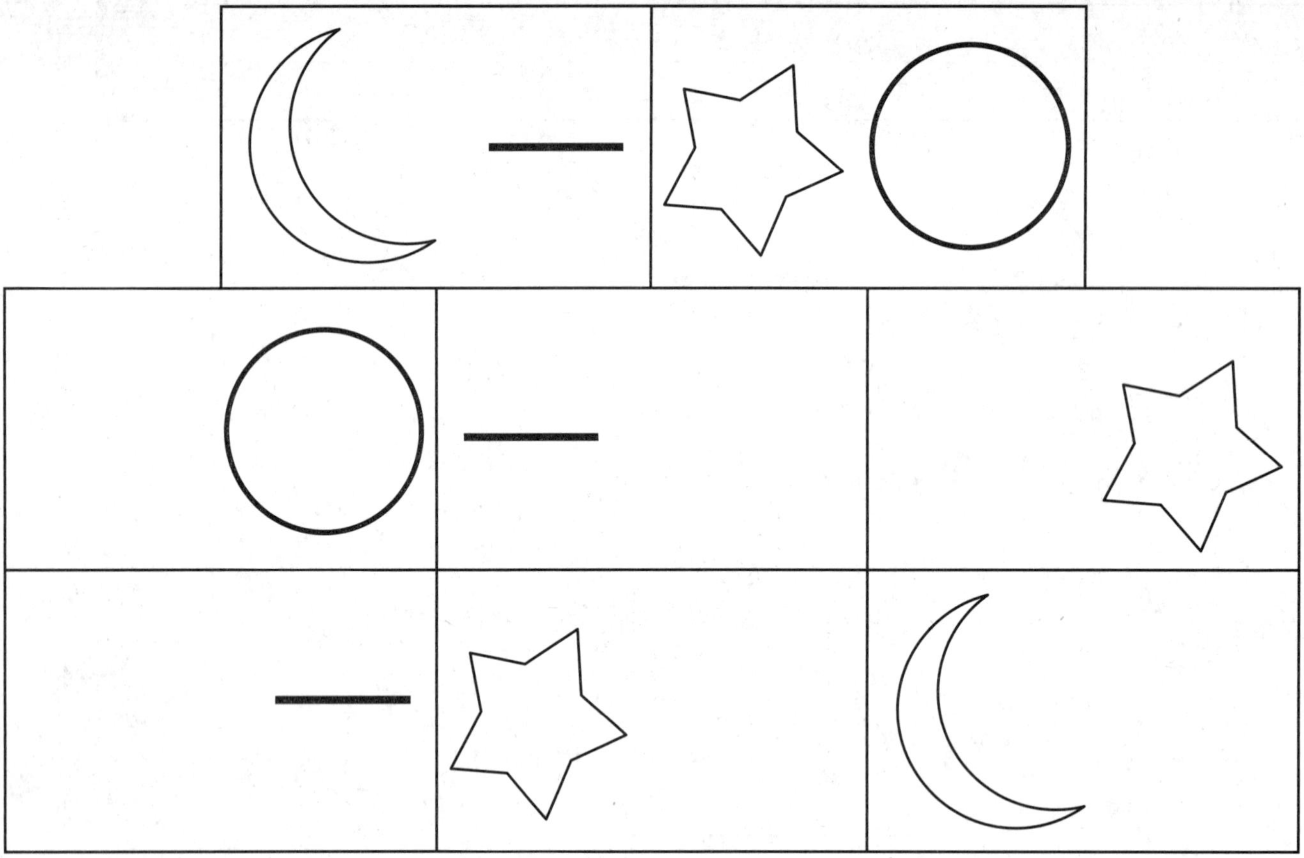

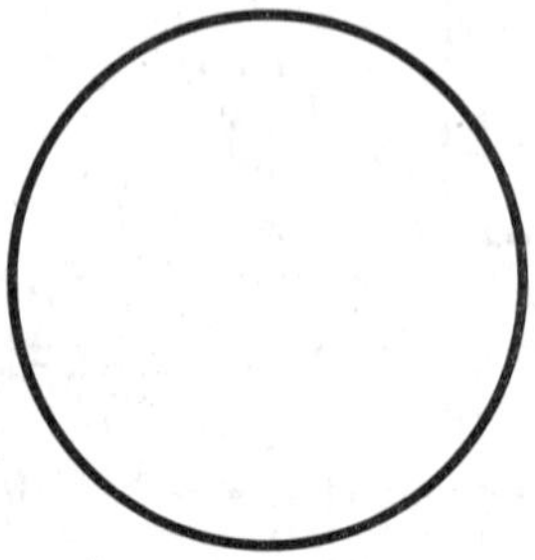

Side 2

| winter | swan | happy |
| funny | fall | ugly | spring |

This fable is about a duck who was really _____

a _____.

The other ducks thought he was _____.

He lived alone in the forest all _____ long.

When spring came, he was _____ to live with the other swans.

I learned that _____.

Side 1

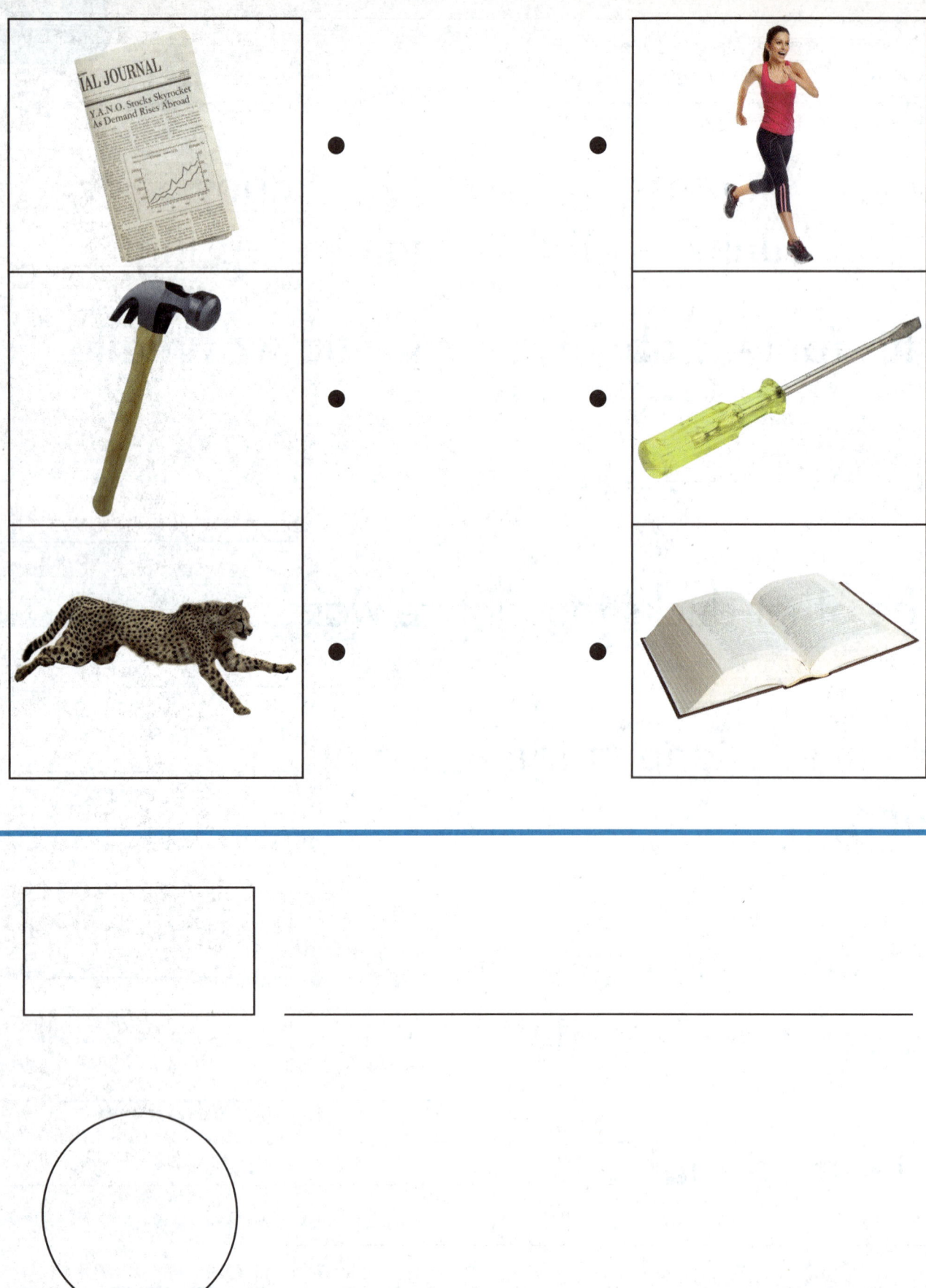

Side 2

Side 2

128

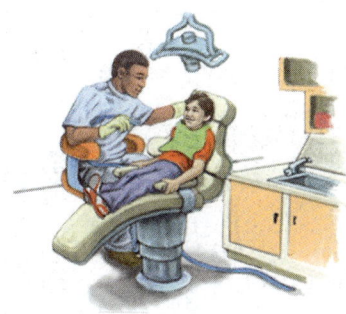  

Side 1

Side 2

129

Side 1

Side 2

130

Side 1

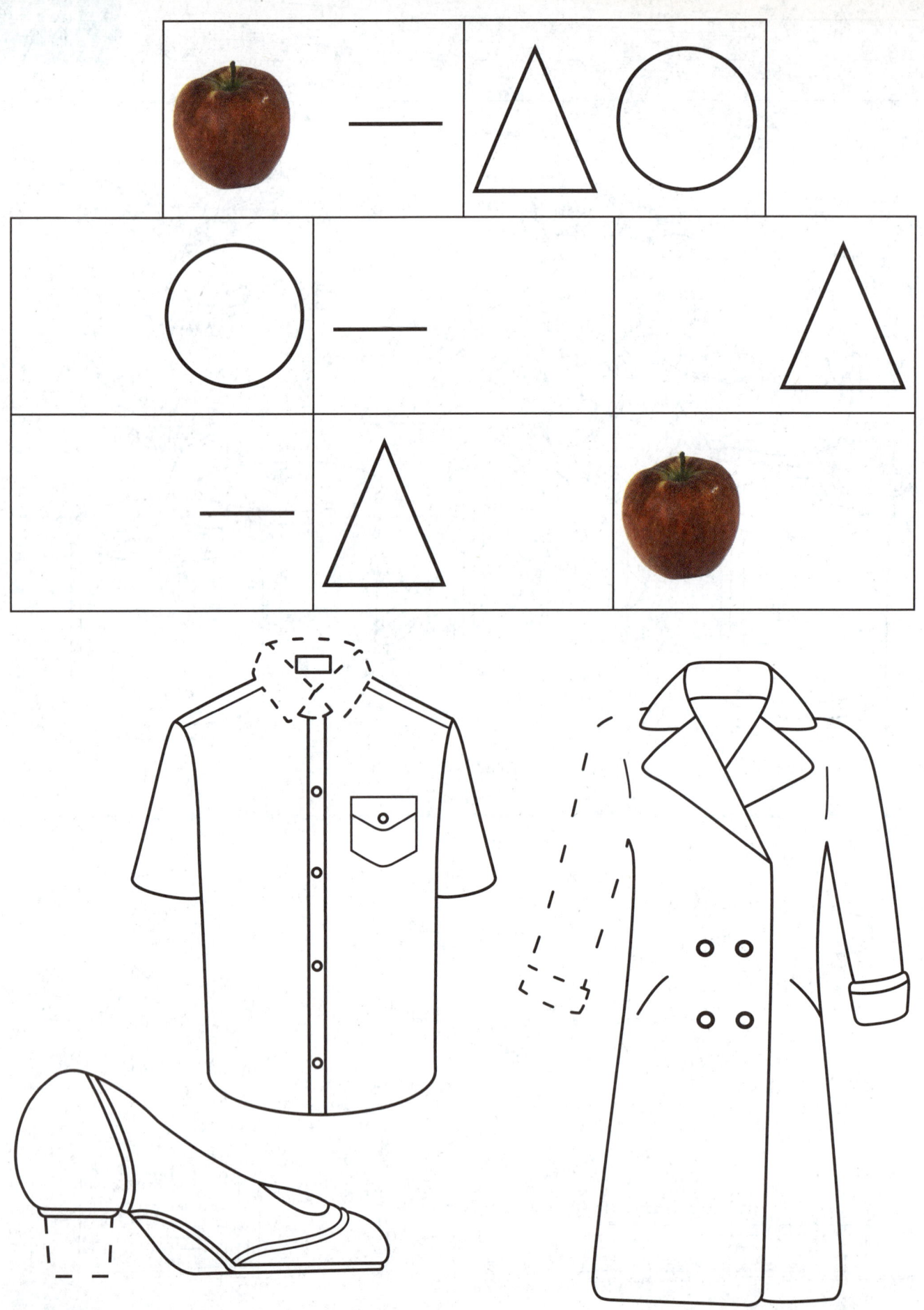

Side 2

_____
_____
_____

pull	grow	build
run jump	find	change

The little pigs had to _____ houses.

Roger had to _____ his hat.

The bragging rats had to _____ down a path to the pond.

The lion had to _____ a thorn out of his paw.

The ugly duckling had to _____ into a swan.

I learned that _____
_____
_____.

Side 2

132

Side 1

Side 2

133

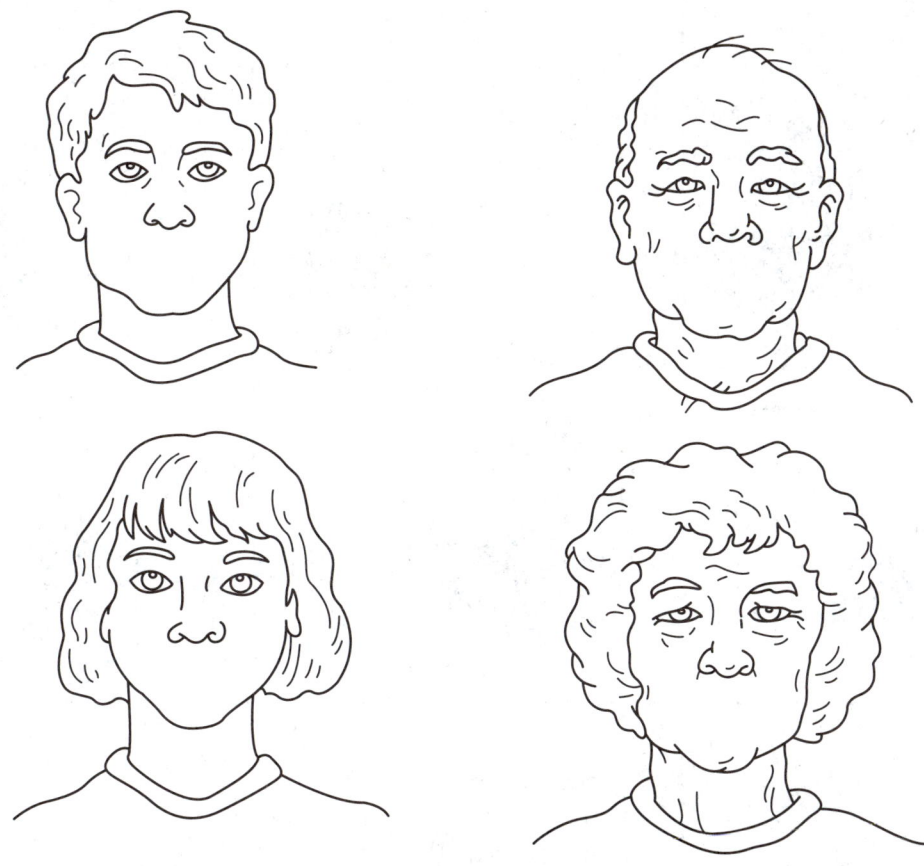

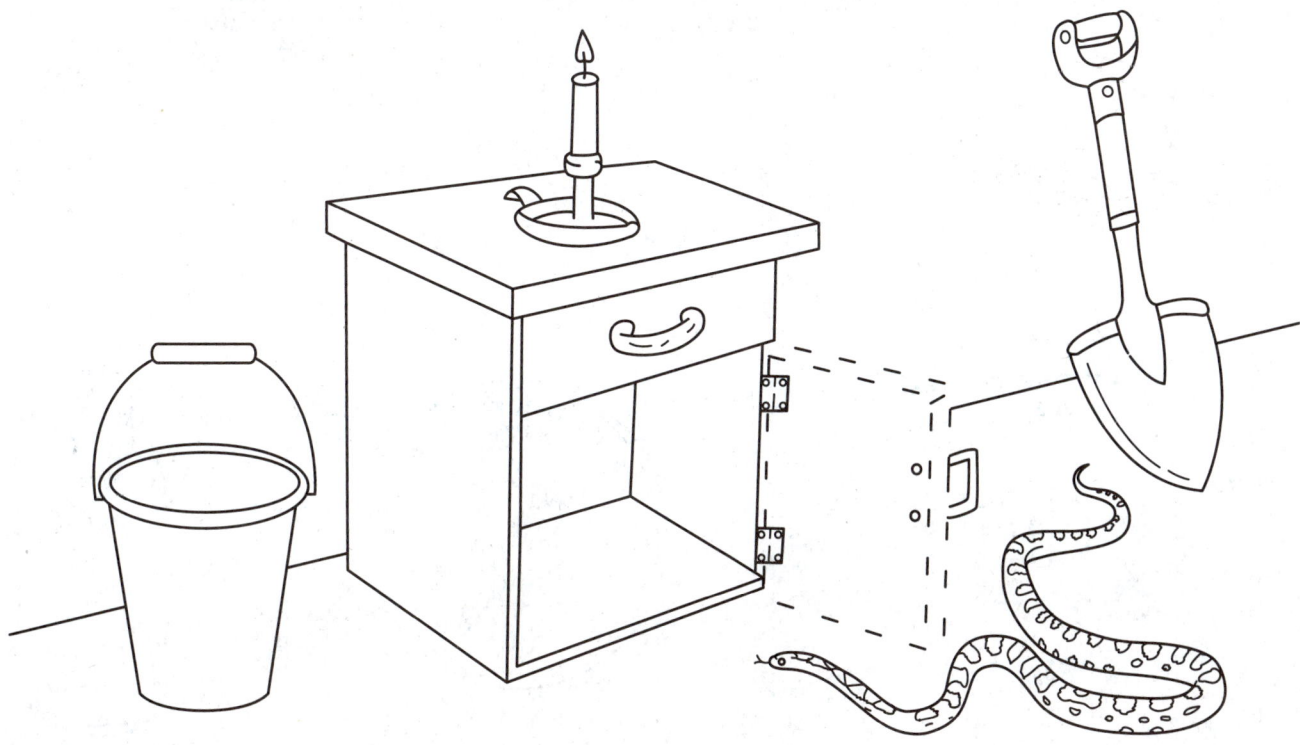

Side 1

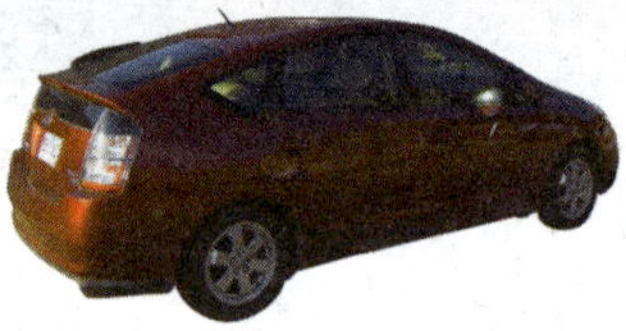 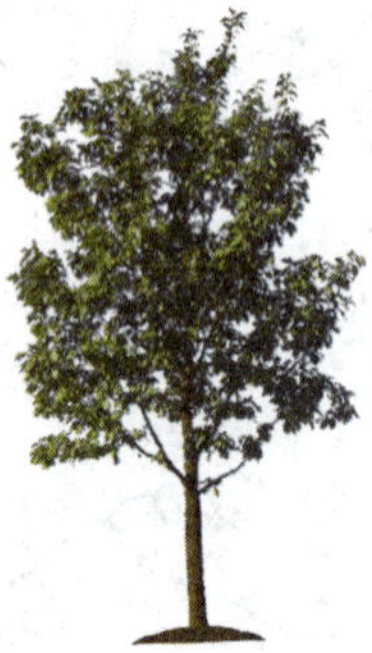 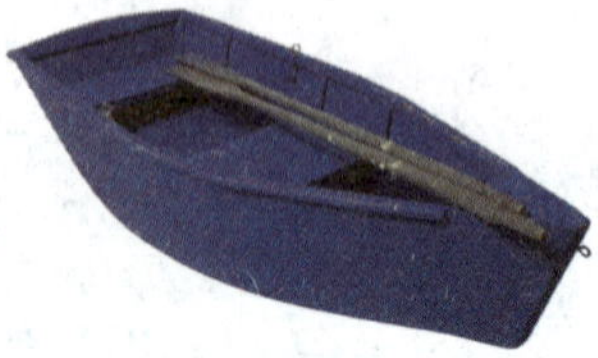	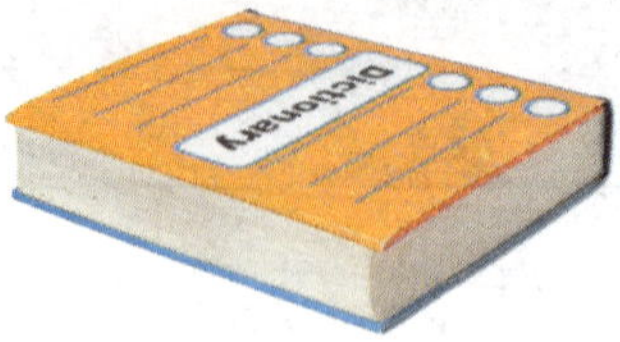 Dictionary 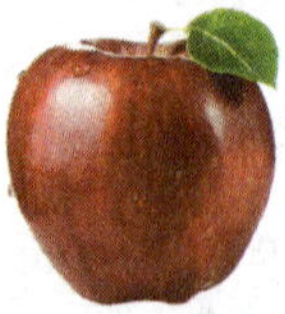 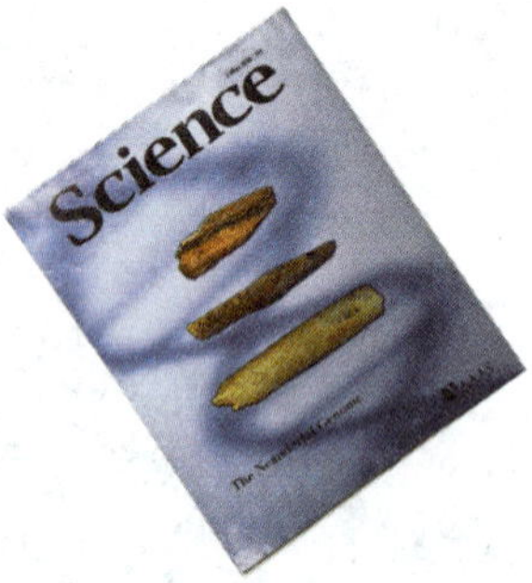 Science	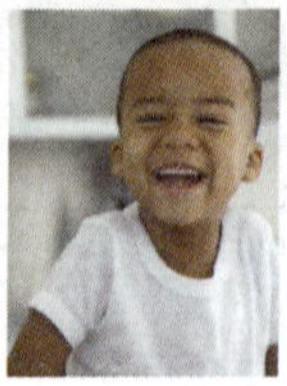 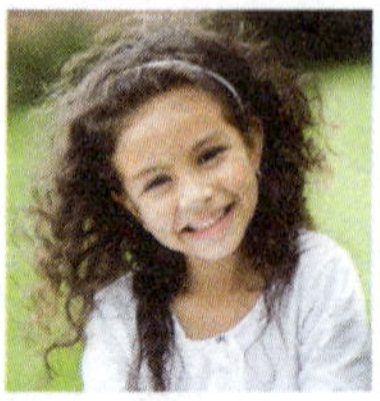 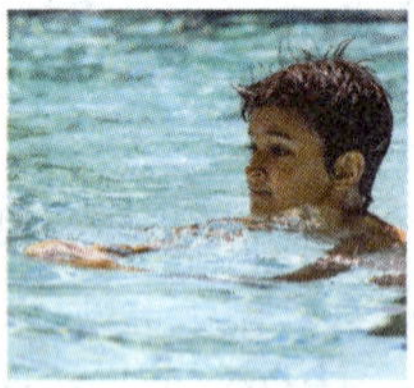

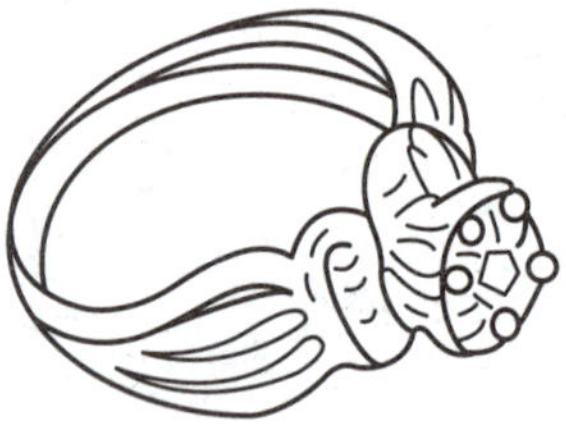

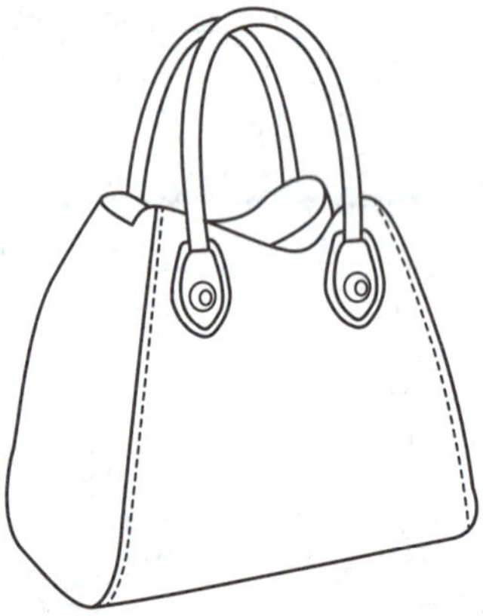

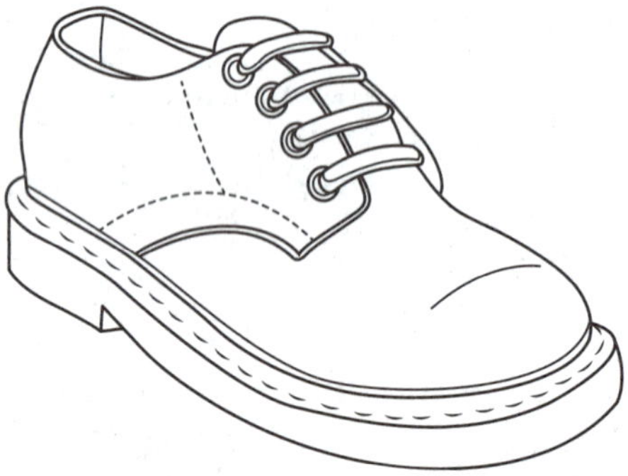

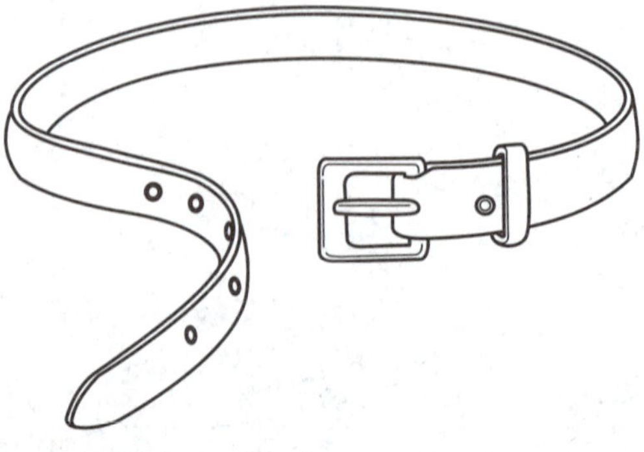

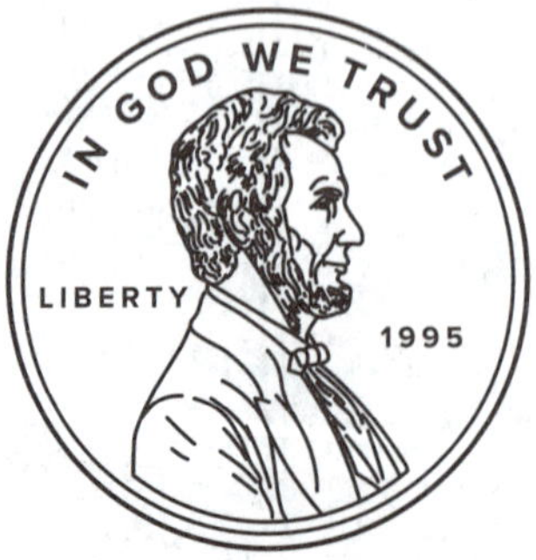
IN GOD WE TRUST
LIBERTY
1995

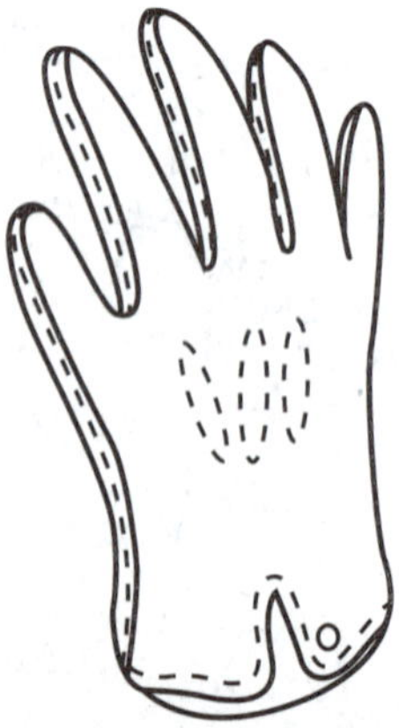

134

Side 1

135

Side 1

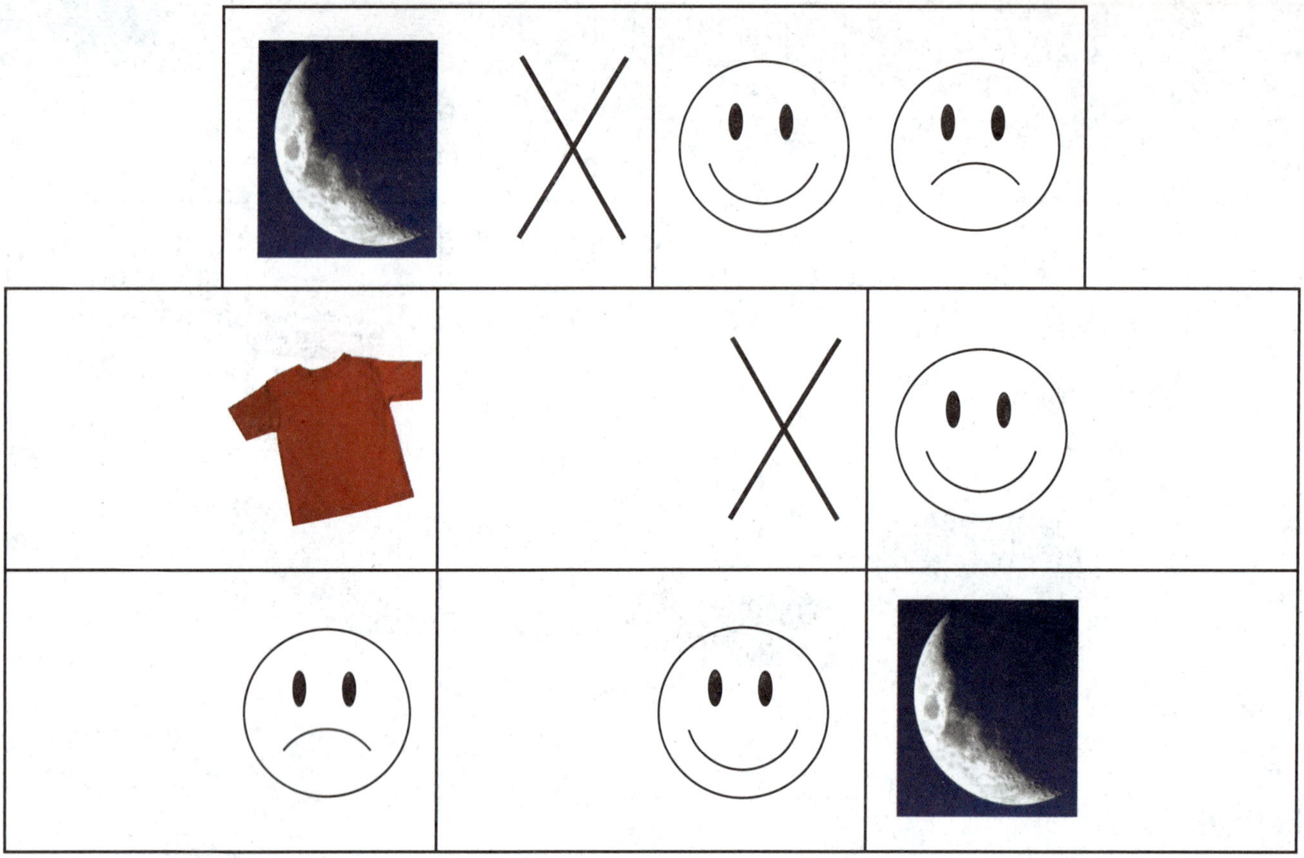

Side 2

136

Side 1

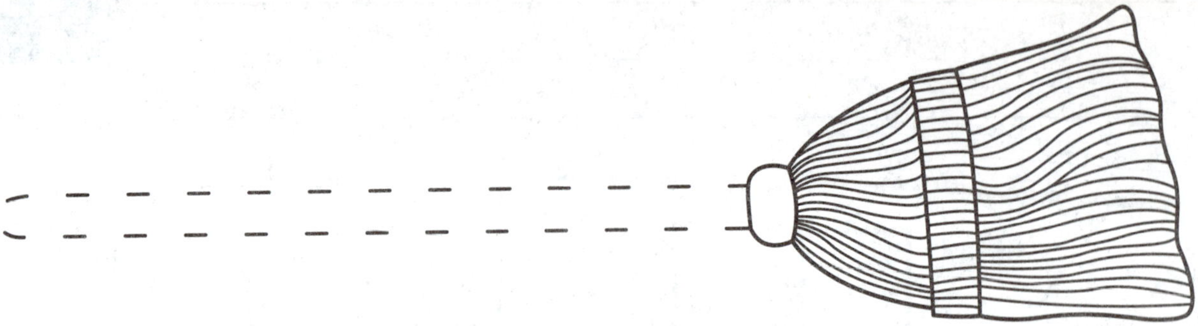

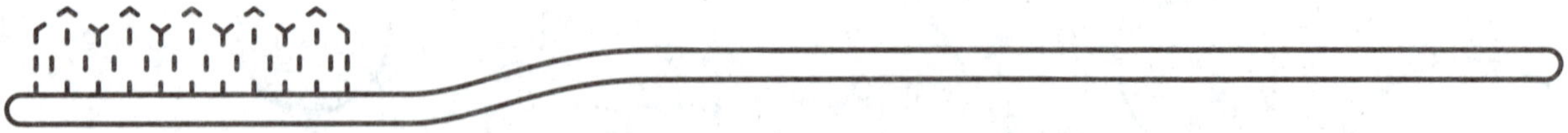

Side 2

137

Side 1

Side 2

red   blue   yellow

green   orange

The color I like most is _____.

The teacher likes _____ the most.

The class likes _____ the most.

We found more _____ things in our classroom.

Side 2

_____
_____

crow

robin

blue jay

owl

hawk

duck

The bird I like most is the
_____
- - - - - - - - - - - - - - -
_____ .

The bird the teacher likes most is the
_____
- - - - - - - - - - - - - - -
_____ .

The bird the class likes most is the
_____
- - - - - - - - - - - - - - -
_____ .

Side 2

_____
_____

140

Paul   the wolf   Sweetie

Roger   Clarabelle   the lion

The class thought that _____ is the funniest character.

The class thought that _____ is the scariest character.

The class thought that _____ is the best character.

The character I like most is _____.

Side 1

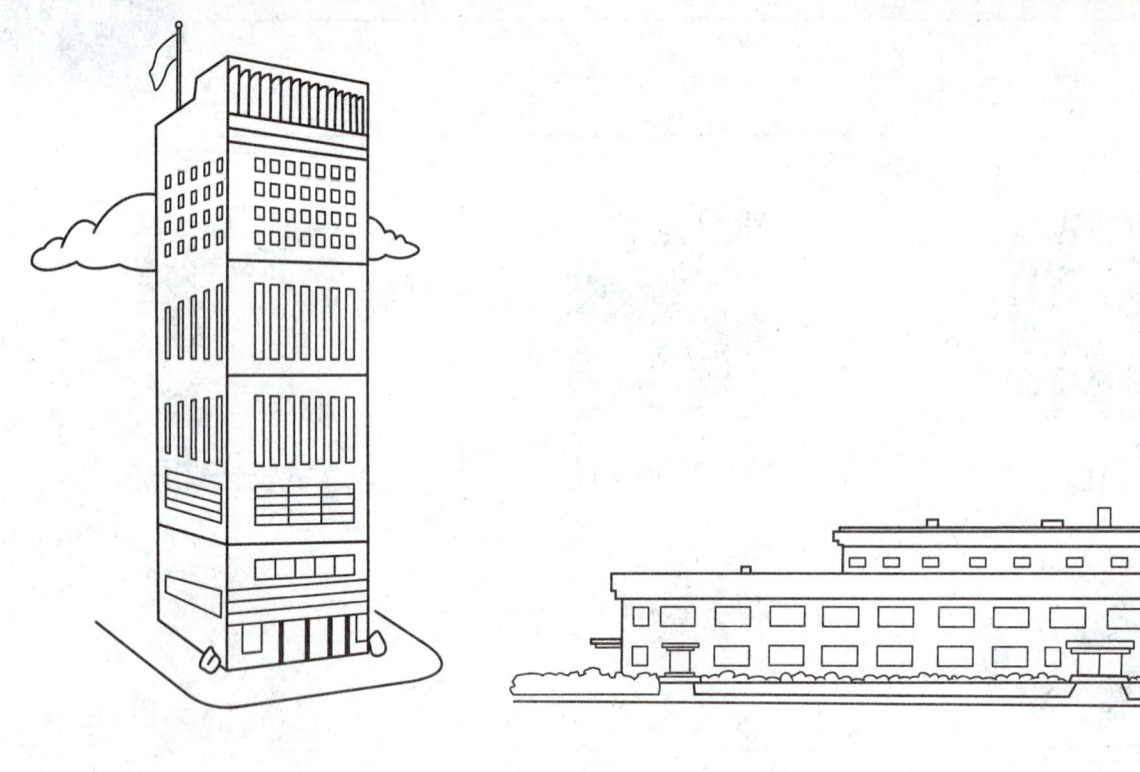

Side 2

_____

wise old rat   princess   little red hen

mouse   ugly duckling   Little Pig 3

The class thought the _____ is very wise.

The class thought the _____ is very brave.

The class thought the _____ is the best character.

I agree / disagree because _____
_____
_____.

Side 1

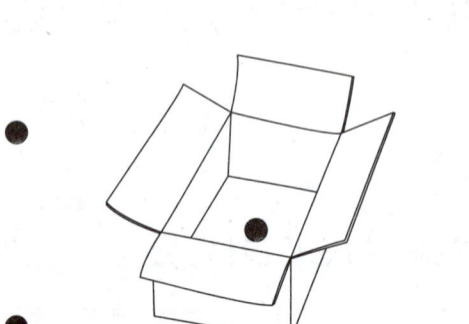

Side 2

143

Side 1

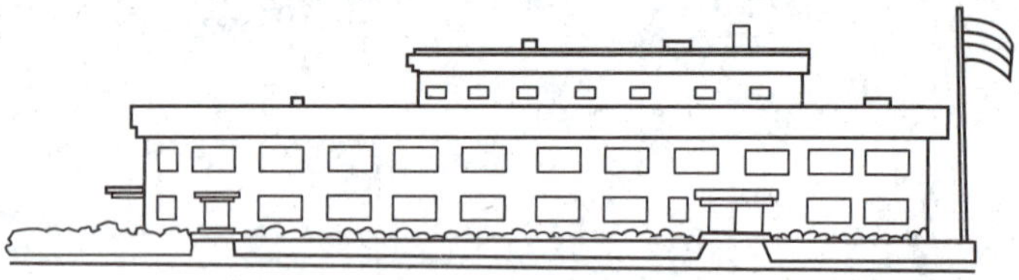

Side 2

144

Side 1

Side 2

| pointed | same | proboscis |
| sharp | different | long |

A butterfly has a _____ to drink nectar from flowers.

Some birds have a _____ beak to drink nectar from flowers.

Baby birds eat the _____ food as adult birds.

A larva and an adult butterfly eat _____ food.

Side 1

Side 2

| seeds | years | eggs | under |
| pollen | over | weeks | shade |

Trees start as _____.

Butterflies start as _____.

Roots grow _____ the ground.

A larva grows _____ the ground.

Trees can live for _____.

Butterflies can live for _____.

Trees make _____ for butterflies.

Butterflies carry _____ for trees.

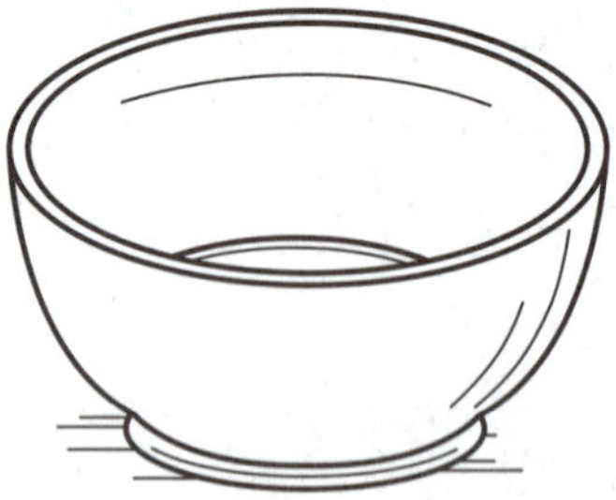

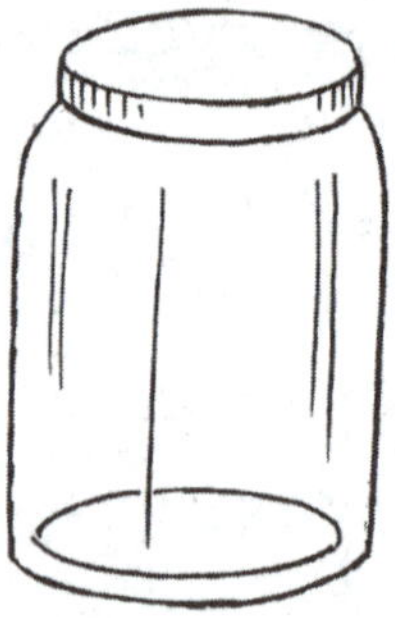

Side 2

147

Side 1

Side 2

_____

winter   spring   summer   fall

The season the class likes most is
_____.

The season the teacher likes most is
_____.

The season I like most is _____.

I like this season most because
_____
_____.

Side 2

forest	jungle	beach
	city	farm

The place the class likes most is a _____.

The place the teacher likes most is a _____.

The place I like most is a _____.

I like this place most because _____.

Side 2

_____
- - - - - - - - - - -
_____

| pointed | short | round | |
| | long | sharp | strong |

Bird beaks are different because
_____
- - - - - - - - - - - - - - - -
_____

_____
_____.

_____
A - - - - - - - - - - - beak helps to catch fish.

_____
A - - - - - - - - - - - beak helps to crack seeds.

_____
A - - - - - - - - - - - beak helps to cut meat.

_____
A - - - - - - - - - - - beak helps to drink nectar.

Side 2

151

STOP EXIT  DANGER

Side 1

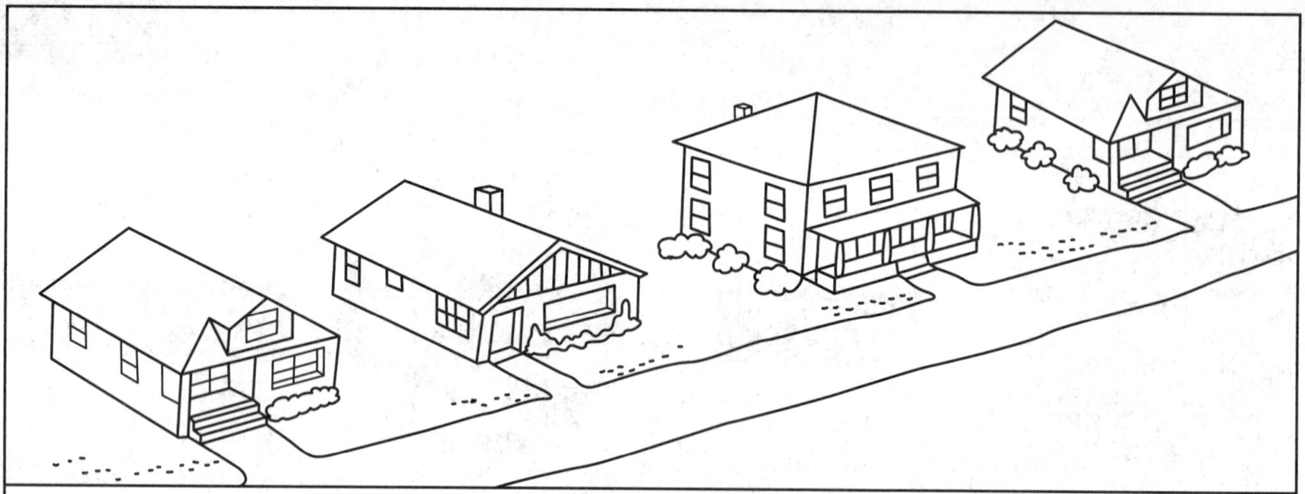

Side 2

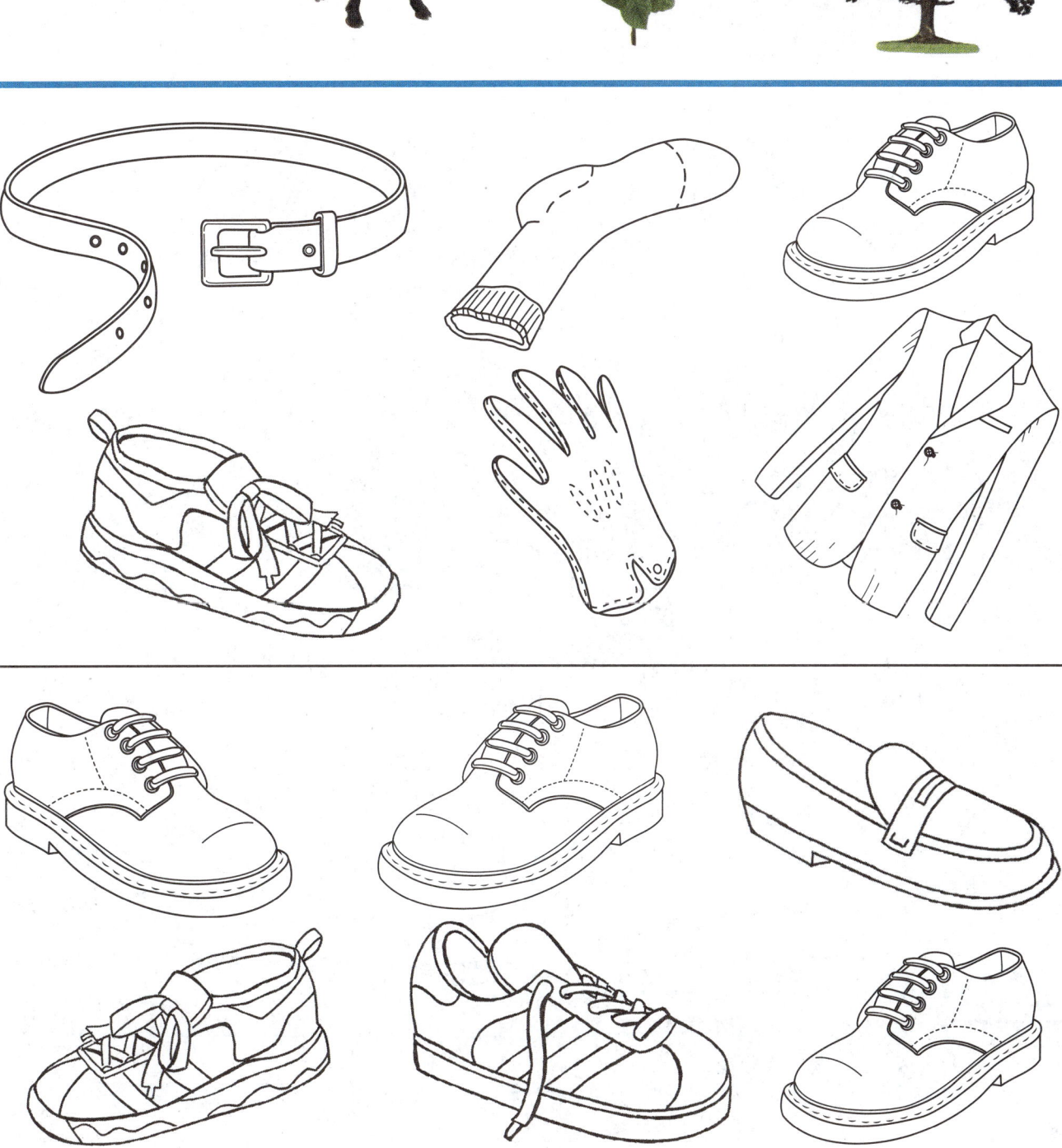

152

Side 1

Side 2

153

Side 1

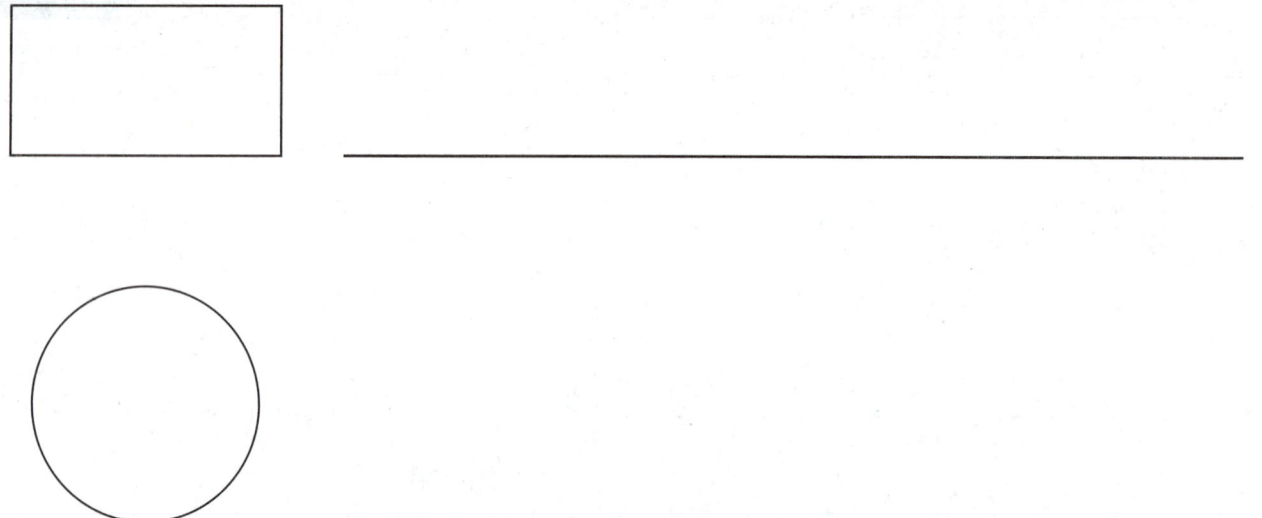

Side 2

154

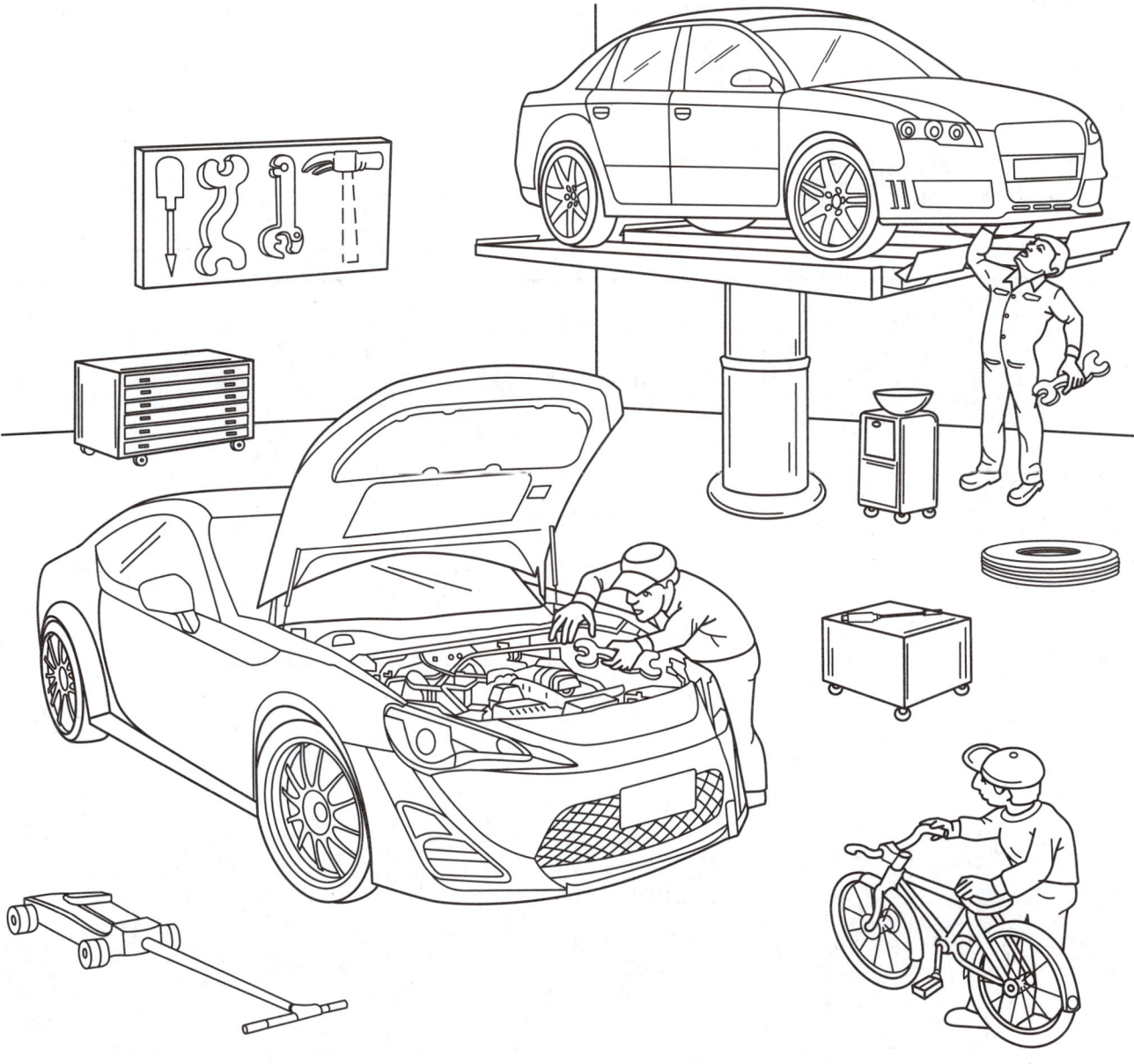

Side 1

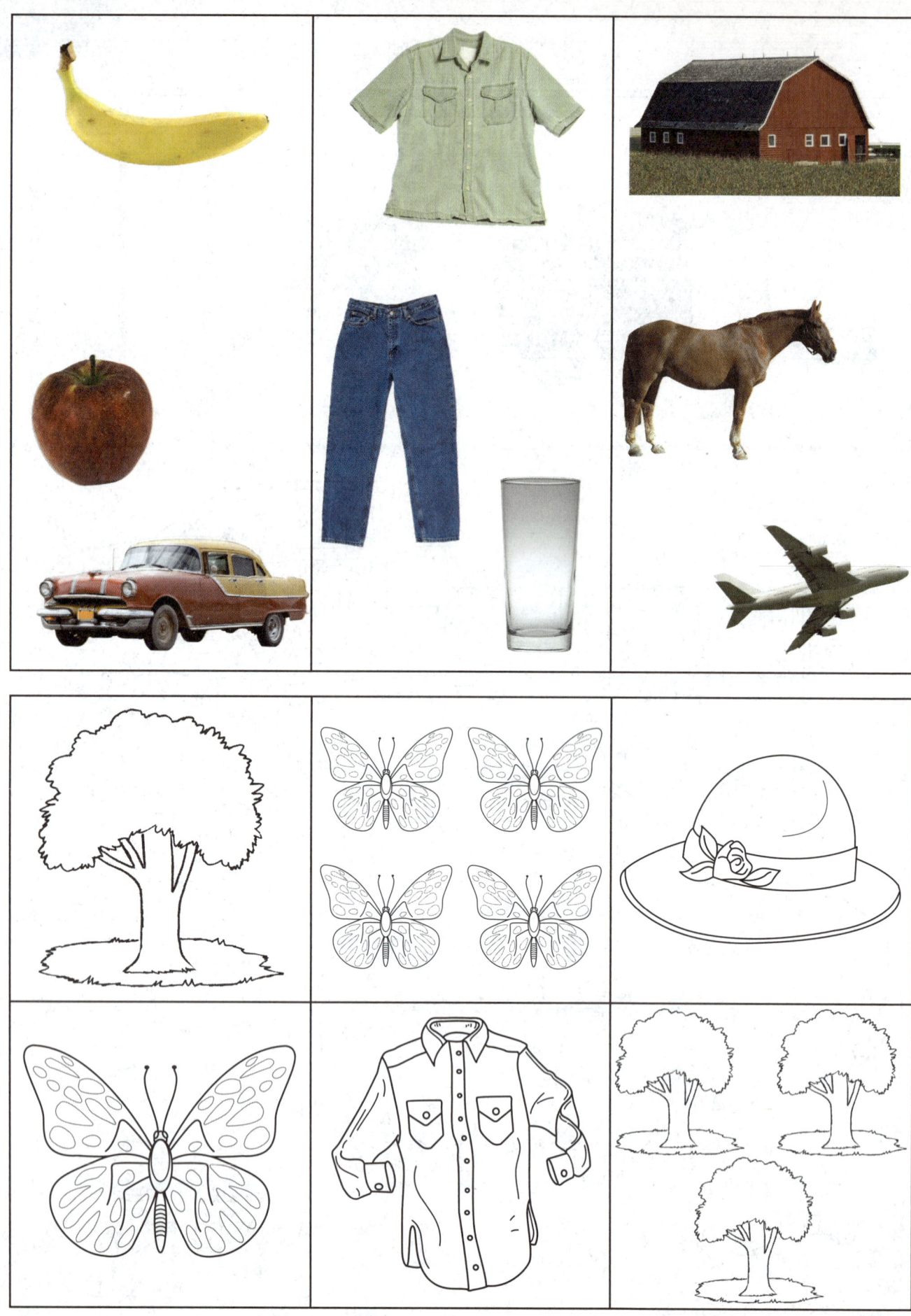

Side 2

  DANGER

PHOTO CREDITS

L081 Side 02 (cap)Iconotec/Glow Images (bottle)Getty Images (fish)Ammit/Getty Images **L082 Side 02** (apple)Author's Image/Glow Images (leaf)©imagebroker/Alamy **L084 Side 02** (baseball)Iconotec/Glow Images (banana)lynx/iconotec.com/Glow Images (rose)©68/Ocean/Corbis (balloon)Ingram Publishing/SuperStock **L085 Side 02** (shoe)Ingram Publishing/SuperStock (hat)Iconotec/Glow Images (fish)Ammit/Getty Images **L087 Side 01** (box)C Squared Studios/Getty Images (apple)Lauren Burke/Photographer's Choice RF/Getty Images (sandwich)gbrundin/E+/Getty Images (cake)©Stockbyte/PunchStock (egg)Clement Mok/Photodisc/Getty Images (bowl)eskaylim/iStockphoto/Getty Images (carrot)PhotoAlto/SuperStock (pail)Ingram Publishing/SuperStock (bottle)Newbird/E+/Getty Images (basket)Shutterstock/Serg64 **L087 Side 02** (baseball)Iconotec/Glow Images (fish)©Wojtek Kalinowski Photography/Corbis (car)Georgii Dolgykh/123RF (broom)Comstock Images/Getty Images **L088 Side 01** (blue bottle)Ingram Publishing/SuperStock (bottle)Getty Images (cup)McGraw Hill/Dot Box Inc. photographer (car)McGraw Hill/Mark Dierker, photographer (yellow bike)©Lawrence Manning/Corbis (bike)©Zoonar GmbH/Alamy (canoe)©Comstock Images/Alamy (plastic cup)McGraw Hill/Mark Steinmetz (suitcase)Oleksiy Maksymenko/Alamy (bowl)Ildi Papp/YAY Micro/age fotostock (airplane)Bim/Getty Images (pail)Ingram Publishing/SuperStock (truck)U.S. Air Force photo by Lisa M. Macias **L089 Side 01** (boat)Randy Lincks/Corbis (bucket)Jan Tadeusz/Alamy (bus)Doug Sherman/Geofile (canoe)Comstock Images/Alamy (box)wabeno/iStock/Getty Images (bottle)Ingram Publishing/SuperStock (bike)Zoonar GmbH/Alamy (cup) McGraw Hill **L089 Side 02** (cup)McGraw Hill (hat)Thinkstock/Alamy **L090 Side 02** (fish)©Wojtek Kalinowski Photography/Corbis (car)McGraw Hill/Mark Dierker, photographer (flag)Tetra Images/Getty Images (boat)Darryl Brooks/Shutterstock **L092 Side 01** (burger)©Ingram Publishing/Alamy (banana)lynx/ iconotec.com/Glow Images (car)Paul Piebinga/Getty Images (boat)Randy Lincks/Corbis (motorcycle)gors4730/123RF (purse)Shutterstock/surasaki (bread)Alex Cao/Getty Images (bag)Mark Steinmetz (pie)DNY59/E+/Getty Images (bus)Fuse/Getty Images (pitcher)Alex Cao/Getty Images (pot)Mark Steinmetz **L092 Side 02** (ball)© McGraw Hill/Jacques Cornell (dog)G.K. & Vikki Hart/Getty Images (kite)D. Hurst/Alamy (cap)Lev Kropotov/Alamy Stock Photo **L097 Side 02** (shoe)Ingram Publishing/SuperStock (dog)G.K. & Vikki Hart/Getty Images **L098 Side 02** (shoe)©Ingram Publishing/Fotosearch (cup)McGraw Hill/Dot Box Inc. photographer (dog)©Ingram Publishing/AGE Fotostock **L102 Side 01** (ship)©NAN/Alamy Stock Photo (egg)©Photodisc/Getty Images (box)wabeno/iStock/Getty Images (apple). Rozenbaum/PhotoAlto (purse)Shutterstock/surasaki (basket)©Ingram Publishing/Alamy (bag)Metta foto/Alamy (bus)Fuse/Getty Images **L103 Side 02** (hat)Iconotec/Glow Images (boat)Randy Lincks/Corbis (bottle)Tony Cordoza/Photographer's Choice RF/Getty Images (butterfly)Shutterstock/M. Shcherbyna **L104 Side 01** (apple)Lauren Burke/Photographer's Choice RF/Getty Images (purse)anouchka/Getty Images (sandwich)Carolyn Taylor Photography/Getty Images (bowl)eskaylim/iStockphoto/Getty Images (mug)McGraw Hill **L104 Side 02** (hat)Iconotec/Glow Images (flower)Shutterstock/Vorobyeva (bottle)thumb/Getty Images (hammer)Comstock Images/Alamy (butterfly)Butterfly Hunter/Shutterstock **L105 Side 01** (boat)Randy Lincks/Corbis (jar)©Markus Guhl/Getty Images (carrot)©Clover/SuperStock (helicopter)imaginewithme/Getty Images (bowl)Ingram Publishing/SuperStock (cheese)Photographer's Choice/Getty Images (bike)aguirre_mar/Getty Images (banana)atoss7/123RF **L109 Side 01** (monkey)Top Photo Engineer/Shutterstock (frog)Digital Vision/PunchStock (cheese)Photographer's Choice/Getty Images (carrot)©Clover/SuperStock (dress)McGraw Hill (coat)Ingram Publishing (belt)Iconotec/Glow Images (bowl)Ildi Papp/YAY Micro/age fotostock **L109 Side 02** (tree)©Lars A. Niki (boat)Darryl Brooks/Shutterstock (shoe)Angelika Antl/age fotostock (flower)Dimitris66/Getty Images **L112 Side 01** (orange cat)G.K. & Vikki Hart/Getty Images (goat)Getty Images/iStockphoto (pig)svetlana foote/123RF (tractor)Getty Images/iStockphoto (dog)McGraw Hill (cat)Grigorita Ko/Shutterstock **L112 Side 02** (banana)lynx/ iconotec.com/Glow Images (cup)McGraw Hill/Dot Box Inc. photographer (hat)Purestock/SuperStock **L113 Side 01** (dog)Sharon Montrose/Getty Images (car)McGraw Hill/Mark Dierker, photographer (shirt)Ingram Publishing (cow)G. K. & Vikki Hart/Photodisc/Getty Images (bowl)eskaylim/iStockphoto/Getty Images (train)qladassfanny/Getty Images (playground)Shutterstock/zstock (swing)sozaijiten/Datacraft/Getty Images (skirt)tarzhanova/123RF **L114 Side 01** (broom)Comstock Images/Getty Images (bat)CrackerClips/Getty Images (toothbrush)©Ingram Publishing/Alamy (rat)Ilia Shcherbakov/123RF (table)Stockbyte/PunchStock (hat)Getty Images/iStockphoto/Amanda Rohde (lion)Shutterstock/Eric Isselee **L114 Side 02** (cap)Iconotec/Glow Images (pencil)McGraw Hill/Ken Karp photographer (broom)Comstock Images/Getty Images (toothbrush)©Ingram Publishing/Alamy (apple)Lauren Burke/Photographer's Choice RF/Getty Images **L119 Side 02** (glass)Andrey_Kuzmin/Getty Images (apple)Author's Image/Glow Images (duck)G.K. & Vikki Hart/Photodisc/Getty Images (broom)Comstock Images/Getty Images (toothbrush)©Ingram Publishing/Alamy **L120 Side 01** (ball)McGraw Hill/Jacques Cornell (cow)G.K. & Vikki Hart/Photodisc/Getty Images (tiger)Shutterstock/nattanan726 (boat)Comstock Images/Alamy (farm)©Steve Hamblin/Alamy (umbrella)Glow Images (leopard)Getty Images (motorcycle)Ingram Publishing/SuperStock (traffic)Lorcan/Digital Vision/Getty Images

L122 Side 02 (shoe)©Ingram Publishing/Fotosearch (bottle)Getty Images (bike)©Lawrence Manning/Corbis (window)Getty Images/iStockphoto (car)Paul Piebinga/Getty Images (hat)©Comstock Images/Alamy (boat)Randy Lincks/Corbis (truck)Andrey Pavlov/Shutterstock (tractor)Getty Images/iStockphoto (bucket)McGraw Hill/Mark Steinmetz (shirt)McGraw Hill (hammer)©Comstock Images/Alamy (plastic cup)McGraw Hill/Mark Steinmetz (bathroom)Siraphol Siricharattakul/EyeEm/Getty Images (brown shoe)C. Zachariasen/PhotoAlto (saddle)©Jules Frazier/Photodisc/Getty Images (dental tool)McGraw Hill/Ken Karp (dental chair)Suljo/iStock/Getty Images **L123 Side 02** (hat)Iconotec/Glow Images (ball)Hutchings Photography/Digital Light Source (glass)Andrey_Kuzmin/Getty Images (toothbrush)©Ingram Publishing/Alamy (apple)Lauren Burke/Photographer's Choice RF/Getty Images **L124 Side 01** (dog)Songphon Kotesopha/123RF (cow)G.K. & Vikki Hart/Photodisc/Getty Images (wagon)C Squared Studios/Photodisc/Getty Images (rag)Sergei Vinogradov/123RF (shirt)McGraw Hill (hammer)©Comstock Images/Alamy (cat)Comstock Images/Alamy (bird)©Design Pics Inc./Alamy (claw hammer)Stockbyte/Getty Images **L126 Side 02** (book)McGraw Hill (hammer)©Comstock Images/Alamy (newspaper)Brand X Pictures/Stockbyte/Getty Images (tool)lynx/iconotec.com/Glow Images (cheetah)Alan and Sandy Carey/Getty Images (runner)Shutterstock/Daxiao Productions **L128 Side 02** (hat)Iconotec/Glow Images (cup)McGraw Hill (apple)Lauren Burke/Photographer's Choice RF/Getty Images **L129 Side 01** (cat)©Ingram Publishing/AGE Fotostock (shoe)©D. Hurst/Alamy (shirt)Ingram Publishing (horse)©Juniors Bildarchiv/Alamy (dog)Songphon Kotesopha/123RF (apple)Author's Image/Glow Images (cow)©Imageshop/Alamy (boat)Comstock Images/Alamy (barn)Steve Hamblin/Alamy **L130 Side 02** (apple)Author's Image/Glow Images (apple)Author's Image/Glow Images (horse)©Juniors Bildarchiv/Alamy (pig)svetlana foote/123RF (hammer)©Comstock Images/Alamy (carrot)PhotoAlto/SuperStock (tool)Yanas/Shutterstock **L133 Side 02** (tree)McGraw Hill (car)McGraw Hill/Mark Dierker, photographer (dictionary)Dot Box Inc./McGraw Hill (boat)Comstock Images/Alamy (boy)Fancy Collection/SuperStock (apple)Lauren Burke/Photographer's Choice RF/Getty Images (magazine)McGraw Hill/Mark Dierker (boy swimming)Shutterstock/Altin Osmanaj (girl)Shutterstock/ESB Professional **L135 Side 01** (shoe)McGraw Hill (window)Richard Goerg/Getty Images (glass)Andrey_Kuzmin/Getty Images (car)©Drazen Vukelic/Getty Images (ship)Medioimages/Superstock (pig)yevgeniy11/Shutterstock (barn)Steve Hamblin/Alamy (shoe)©Anton Starikov/Alamy Stock Photo (helicopter)imaginewithme/Getty Images **L135 Side 02** (shirt)Studiohio (moon)©Eyebyte/Alamy **L137 Side 02** (hat)Iconotec/Glow Images (flower)Martin Ruegner/Getty Images (tree)Lars A. Niki (boat)Randy Lincks/Corbis (bottle)Newbird/E+/Getty Images (butterfly)©Ingram Publishing/AGE Fotostock **L139 Side 01** (duck)Juniors Bildarchiv/Alamy (crow)McGraw Hill (robin)William Leaman/Alamy (blue jay)©James Urbach/SuperStock (owl)©Erwin & Peggy Bauer/Corbis (hawk)McGraw Hill/Mark Dierker **L142 Side 01** (shoe)©Ingram Publishing/Fotosearch (door)Design Pics/Carson Ganci (goat)Dmitri Gomon/Shutterstock (jeans)C Squared Studios/Getty Images (coat)McGraw Hill **L143 Side 01** (cowboy hat)Iconotec/Glow Images (broom)Comstock Images/Getty Images (toothbrush)Shevchuk Boris/iStockphoto/Getty Images (rake)lynx/ iconotec.com/Glow Images **L144 Side 01** (umbrella)©Ingram Publishing/Fotosearch (house)Ryan McVay/Photodisc/Getty Images (wagon)C Squared Studios/Photodisc/Getty Images (broom)Comstock Images/Getty Images **L145 Side 02** (bike)Creative Crop/Getty Images (umbrella)©Ingram Publishing/Fotosearch (wagon)C Squared Studios/Photodisc/Getty Images (boat)Randy Lincks/Corbis **L147 Side 01** (BMX bike)Creative Crop/Getty Images (bike)Fuse/Getty Images (elephant)McGraw Hill (sandwich)Carolyn Taylor Photography/Stockbyte/Getty Images (wagon)C Squared Studios/Photodisc/Getty Images (boat)Darryl Brooks/Shutterstock (train)©Image Source Plus/Alamy Stock Photo (umbrella)©Ingram Publishing/Alamy (apple)Lauren Burke/Photographer's Choice RF/Getty Images (butterfly)Studio-Annika/Getty Images **L147 Side 02** (shoe)©Ingram Publishing/Fotosearch (cup)McGraw Hill (book)Dot Box Inc./McGraw Hill (frog)Digital Vision/PunchStock **L148 Side 02** (table)McGraw Hill (car)Georgii Dolgykh/123RF (sofa)Pix11/Shutterstock (chair)Ingram Publishing **L149 Side 02** (coat)McGraw Hill (cat)McGraw Hill (shirt)Ingram Publishing (can)Jeffrey Coolidge/Photodisc/Getty Images **L150 Side 02** (wagon)David Buffington/Getty Images (saw)McGraw Hill/Mark Steinmetz (hammer)©Comstock Images/Alamy (rake)lynx/iconotec/Glow Images **L152 Side 01** (tree)Perfect Picture Parts/Alamy (rose)©68/Ocean/Corbis (goat)Dmitri Gomon/Shutterstock (log)Lev Kropotov/Shutterstock **L152 Side 02** (cat)G.K. & Vikki Hart/Getty Images (fish)©Wojtek Kalinowski Photography/Corbis (kite)D. Hurst/Alamy (leaf)©imagebroker/Alamy (apple)Lauren Burke/Photographer's Choice RF/Getty Images **L154 Side 01** (window)Getty Images/iStockphoto (glass)Andrey_Kuzmin/Getty Images (suitcase)D. Hurst/Alamy (pail)Ingram Publishing/SuperStock **L154 Side 02** (banana)lynx/iconotec.com/Glow Images (horse)©Ingram Publishing/Alamy (car)©Drazen Vukelic/Getty Images (apple)Author's Image/Glow Images (glass)©RelaXimages/Corbis (shirt)McGraw Hill (airplane)Bim/Getty Images (jeans)C Squared Studios/Getty Images (barn)Philip Coblentz/age fotostock **L155 Side 02** (cup)Iconotec/Glow Images (clock)Ingram Publishing (shirt)Studiohio (balloon)Ingram Publishing/SuperStock (book)Dot Box Inc./McGraw Hill